**FALCON**GUIDE®

Rock Climbing the San Francisco Bay Area

by Tresa Black

 **FALCON**GUIDES®

GUILFORD, CONNECTICUT
HELENA, MONTANA
AN IMPRINT OF THE GLOBE PEQUOT PRESS

Λ FALCON GUIDE ®

Copyright © 2002 Morris Book Publishing, LLC

Falcon, FalconGuides,. and Chockstone are registered trademarks of Morris Book Publishing, LLC.

Page design by Gloria Serena
Photo bases for photo topos are by the author unless otherwise noted.
Interior photos are by the author unless otherwise noted.
Maps by Sue Cary © Morris Book Publishing, LLC

Library of Congress Cataloging-in-Publication Data is available.
Black, Tresa.
   Rock climbing San Francisco / Tresa Black. — 1st ed.
      p. cm. — (A FalconGuide)
   ISBN 978-0-7627-1143-7
   Calif.)—Guidebooks. I. Title. II. Falcon guide

GV199.42.C2 S353 2002
796.52'23'09794—dc21   2002074242

Printed in the United States of America
First Edition/Fourth Printing

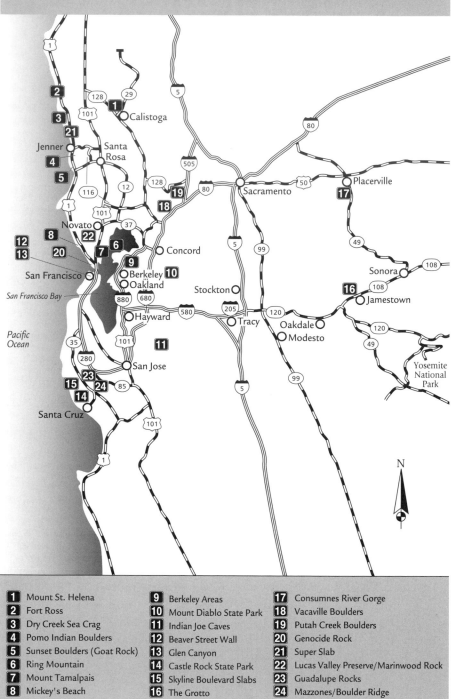

SAN FRANCISCO BAY AREA

1 Mount St. Helena
2 Fort Ross
3 Dry Creek Sea Crag
4 Pomo Indian Boulders
5 Sunset Boulders (Goat Rock)
6 Ring Mountain
7 Mount Tamalpais
8 Mickey's Beach
9 Berkeley Areas
10 Mount Diablo State Park
11 Indian Joe Caves
12 Beaver Street Wall
13 Glen Canyon
14 Castle Rock State Park
15 Skyline Boulevard Slabs
16 The Grotto
17 Consumnes River Gorge
18 Vacaville Boulders
19 Putah Creek Boulders
20 Genocide Rock
21 Super Slab
22 Lucas Valley Preserve/Marinwood Rock
23 Guadalupe Rocks
24 Mazzones/Boulder Ridge

Contents

Preface vii

Acknowledgments ix

INTRODUCTION 1
  A Brief Climbing History 2
  Topo Key 4
  How to Use This Book....................5
  Rating Systems for Technical Climbs....5
  Rating Systems for Bouldering 6

NORTH BAY AREAS......................9
  Mount St. Helena......................9
  Fort Ross Boulders....................27
  Dry Creek Sea Crag 31
  Pomo Indian Boulders 43
  Sunset Boulders (Goat Rock)...........47
  Ring Mountain 52
  Mount Tamalpais......................59
  Mickey's Beach 69

EAST BAY AND
SAN FRANCISCO AREAS 89
  Berkeley Areas.......................89
  Mount Diablo State Park 105
  Indian Joe Caves 121
  Beaver Street Wall 127
  Glen Canyon 133

SOUTH BAY AREAS 139
  Castle Rock State Park 139
  Skyline Boulevard Slabs 165

EAST OF THE BAY AREAS 171
  The Grotto.............................171
  Consumnes River Gorge 184
  Vacaville Boulders 196
  Putah Creek Boulders 201

OTHER AREAS 206
  Genocide Rock 206
  Super Slab 207
  Lucas Valley/Marinwood Rock 209
  Guadalupe Rocks 211
  Mazzones/Boulder Ridge 213

Appendix: Climbing Gyms 215

Rated Route Index 217

Route Name Index 223

About the Author 229

Preface

It was a beautiful sunny day in February of 2000 and I was excited to get outside and do some climbing. Nearly every one of my days off in the past month had been spoiled by inclement weather, which left me pulling on plastic at the gym instead of enjoying the outdoors. Today, however, the weather was perfect with bright skies, mild temperatures, and a slight cool wind that promised to wick the sweat from my fingertips when I climbed.

My climbing partner Bill and I gathered up the gear and hit the road to a nearby destination we had only been to twice. Leaving the house at 7:00 A.M., we planned on a leisurely hour-and-a-half drive (coffee break included) before arriving at the trailhead that led to the site.

Since we were planning on climbing a wall we previously had not been to, we figured the hike to the crag would take an extra 15 to 20 minutes. With this in mind (as well as the new routefinding involved), we speculated that we would be climbing by 10:00 A.M. for sure. We would be good and tired by 4:00 P.M. when I estimated we would need to hit the road due to pet-feeding obligations I had back at home.

Au contraire. To make a very long, arduous story short, it took us an additional hour to find the wall, and nearly as long to decipher which routes were which. Several routes were there but not listed or even mentioned in the current Bay Area guide. We wondered what the difficulty rating was for the route we were hopping on. Were the bolts good up top? Although the bottom half of the route appeared to be good 5.10 climbing, what was the second half of the climb like? Albeit the day was productive and injury-free, I actually climbed about half the time intended.

On the way home we discussed writing a new guide, and since it has always been hard for me to refuse a dare, I promised to get my tush in gear and write the book. Once I realized the commitment I had just made, I wanted to either eat my words or somehow give Bill amnesia. How can I back out on this now, I thought? It was too late. Bill had already started in on new ideas for the book and stated how excited he was that I was going to put it all together.

The ironic thing about this project is that the more work I completed, the more work I found that needed to be done. What I thought would take me six months ended up taking me fourteen! I researched information, drew topos, took pictures, climbed a majority of the routes in the book, and wrote text because I thought there was a real need for a comprehensive guide that would benefit all types of climbers that reside and visit the Bay Area.

Writing this book has changed my life and opened the door to new discoveries . . . good and not so good. Despite the amazing strength and feats of Lynn Hill and other female climbers, the climbing community is not immune to sexism. There are some men that do not believe a woman can write a climbing guidebook, or furthermore actually climb the majority of the routes in the book. Ironically enough, these few men with their disparaging comments and sarcastic words of advice actually helped me write the book because I needed to disprove their theories about women. Overall, I received overwhelming support from climbers in the Bay Area, and I really cannot give enough thanks to all the fine people who helped me and believed I could and would finish *Rock Climbing in the San Francisco Bay Area*.

Acknowledgments

A thousand thank yous to geologist Larry Guenther, who made repeated trips to many of the crags and answered my endless e-mails and phone calls regarding the type of rock and how the heck it got there. Endless thanks to Chris Summit and Richie Esquibel for their invaluable help on many of the North Bay climbing areas, including Fort Ross, Dry Creek, Mount St. Helena, Super Slab, and Mickey's Beach, just to name a few. Also thanks to Kenny Ariza who was always positive and supportive and gave me a great deal of help with Mickey's Beach; Lynn Cuthbertson for climbing with me and continually catching my numerous falls, as well as being a great friend; Eric Brand for Mickey's Beach and historical information of the Bay Area; Ross MacKenzie for climbing with me when all he really wanted to do was boulder; Jim Cope and Rich Fettke, the East Bay Climbing Posse, who offered encouragement and plenty of belays; Steve Roper for help with the Berkeley areas, as well as positive feedback; Allen Steck for valuable Berkeley information; Mark Howe for a wealth of information on Dry Creek and Mount St. Helena; Ken Stanton for route information at the Far Side at Mount St. Helena; Brian Hirchert for a huge amount of help with photos when he knew my cash flow was barely trickling; Kevin Beneda, Craig McClenahan, and Erica McClenahan for their help with routes at the Grotto; Derek Powell for help with Mickey's Beach and bouldering in Berkeley, as well as skipping out on work to climb; Edwin Drummond for Mount Diablo information; Nick Fain who helped produce some great photos of the Egg at Mickey's Beach, as well as doing some badly needed "fixing-up" work on other images; Rick Ford, another knowledge-able geologist, for helping me with rock descriptions and climbing with me even though I had "an agenda"; Russell Bobzien for his quality photos and historical information on Ring Mountain and Mickey's Beach; Caledonia Camera in Sausalito for giving me great deals on prints; Terry Goyan for Grotto photos; Sepand Joorabchi for his valiant mud-slogging efforts while crag hunting with me; and Rita Granados for taking care of my ornery pot-bellied pig, Guiseppe, when I was constantly gone climbing.

I also appreciate the awesome Consumnes Chick Crew: Sue Dziedzic, Karen Evansen, and Kathryn Hayes. Many thanks to the current Castle Rock guidebook author, Bruce Morris, who was not only helpful but also very modest. In addition, a big thank you to guidebook authors, William Cottrell (Consumnes River Gorge) and Grant Hiskes (The Grotto). I can't forget to thank the staff, especially Rebecca and Ted, at Class 5 Fitness in San Rafael for all their help getting contact names and phone numbers; and of course, thanks to all the climbers who made themselves available for photos.

Without the help and encouragement of Jenni Black, Leeta Steenwyk, and Gail Weissman, Ankra Sira, and of course my mom, who knows how many marbles would be rolling around my feet right now. Muchas Gracias Senoritas! And of course, I cannot forget to thank the ever patient and sweet Bill Granados who gave me the idea for writing the book, helped me edit it, and continually came to my rescue with either computer support or general freak out support.

Colin Solomon on Tree Surgeon, *Summit Rock, Castle Rock State Park*

Introduction

Climbing in the Bay Area is much like its culture, unique and diverse. Take a look at the multitude of restaurants available within a mile radius in San Francisco. Mediterranean, Cajun, Japanese, Basque, German, and Thai, to name only a few. Bounded by vineyards in the north (which produce some of the best wine in the world) and Silicon Valley in the south (which changes the face of Wall Street on a daily basis), San Francisco Bay is surrounded by a colorful assortment of complex landscapes and rare ecology.

The diversified weather patterns are proof of the intricate nature of "The City by the Bay." Our lack of tornadoes, tsunamis, snowstorms, intense humidity, and thunderstorms mean more quality climbing days throughout the year. All in all the usual "mild" weather around the San Francisco Bay draws thousands of tourists to area attractions year-round, but at the same time on a given day temperatures can range from a cool 50 degrees in San Francisco to a scorching 90-plus degrees in several inland areas.

Northern California geology is extremely complicated and distinctive, and although many questions are unanswered, we are aware of the brilliance and magnificence the rocks in the Bay Area offer. The variance of rock in the Bay Area is also vast, and therefore the climbing is as well. To the north, volcanic tuff juts out from the mountainous, fertile, wine country. Along the coast, north of San Francisco green and blue schist (often littered with garnets) is common, and greywacke is mingled with golden sandstone. Colorful chert is familiar rock, as well as serpentine—the state rock of California. Wide varieties of basalts and several types of shales, jadeites, and rhyolites call the Bay Area their home.

You will rarely find any of the Bay Area crags crowded if you are fortunate enough to set aside a few weekdays every-so-often for climbing. There are numerous possibilities within a short drive of the Bay. Weekends may be congested, depending on the season and area you visit. Certain sections of the Berkeley Areas, Castle Rock State Park, Ring Mountain, Goat Rock (Sunset Boulders), and Mount Diablo experience a good deal of traffic, and you may need to take a number and wait for a well-known route or boulder problem.

If you are looking for fine bouldering, excellent rock and problems await you in nearly every county surrounding San Francisco. Castle Rock State Park in the South Bay, Indian Rock in the East Bay, Mickey's Beach in the North Bay, just to name a few.

Is steep sport climbing your passion? Great sport possibilities are surely within an hour drive of you regardless of whether your home is north, south, or east of the city. There are actually a fair number of good cracks to jam your way up in the Bay Area. Rack up at Mount Diablo, Castle Rock, Consumnes River Gorge, or The Grotto. Why wait for the weekend to climb?

A Brief Climbing History

Since its legendary rocks are within the close proximity to the San Francisco Bay Area, it is not surprising that many of Yosemite National Park's first ascentionists resided in and sharpened their skills in the Bay Area.

The Sierra Club, chartered in San Francisco in 1924, played a huge role in budding Bay Area climbing. In 1931, a young Cal Berkeley law student named Dick Leonard formed the Cragmont Climbing Club from the San Francisco Bay Area chapter of the Sierra Club. Along with Leonard, climbing greats such as Jules Eichorn and David Brower practiced climbing techniques at Indian Rock, Cragmont, and Remillard in Berkeley. In fact, Brower and Leonard practiced climbing at the Berkeley rocks for two years before they were confident they had the proper skills to tackle a square inch of the mighty Yosemite granite. Some other worthy names who contributed to rock climbing around the Bay: Bill Horsfall, Hervey Voge, and Marj Farquhar. Farquhar also wrote about and filmed a variety of climbing excursions. Although the Berkeley area was probably the most frequented Bay Area destination at the time, the Sierra Club members and friends also visited Castle Rock State Park (north of Santa Cruz), Glen Canyon (in San Francisco), Mount Diablo (east of San Francisco), as well as the Stinson and Mickey's Beach rocks.

The Sierra Club's climbing excursions were temporarily brought to a standstill due to World War II as more than 1,000 club members served in the war effort. Many members saw combat with the U.S. Mountain Troops, and a good portion of the Army manual, *Mountain Operations*, was compiled by David Brower and the Sierra Club.

Allen Steck joined the Berkeley climbing craze in the 1940s and like many of his peers made climbing the core of his existence. Among his many achievements: the first ascent of Hummingbird Ridge on Mount Logan in Canada (this full climb has not yet been repeated), first ascent of Paiju Peak in Pakistan, and the luminous Steck-Salathé in Yosemite.

Frank Sarnquist, David Brower, Raffi Bedayn, and other Sierra Club members sustained fresh climbing in the 1950s. In 1954 at the age of thirteen, the introverted, yet bewildered Steve Roper took part in the Sierra Club outings every Sunday at 1 P.M. The once-reticent Roper emerged from his shell and discovered the world of climbing—soon to become his life-long passion. Ten years later Roper published the first comprehensive guide to rock climbing in the Yosemite Valley. Roper also touched-off the "need for speed," with the first single-day speed ascent of Half Dome in Yosemite in 1966. An American Alpine Club Literary Award Winner, Roper authored several books, most notably *Camp 4: Recollections of a Yosemite Rockclimber* and *50 Classic Climbs of North America*.

Galen Rowell, often referred to as the Master of Berkeley's Indian Rock, also frequented Mickey's Beach and Split Rock (in the north bay) in the 1960s along with Ron Kauk, Ehren Feucht, Les Wilson, and Peter Haan were also instrumental in pioneering numerous routes around the Bay in the early 1960s. These areas included various Marin County locales as well as Hunter's Hill in Vallejo, (currently on private property and off limits to climbers and hikers).

Brock Wagstaff of Marin County launched his climbing career in the early 1970s in his early teens. He and his comrade Rob Boyd decided to give climbing a go on local rock near Cataract Falls in Fairfax. Unsure of the proper *modus operandi*, Wagstaff used 20-penny nails to aid climb the rock in his hiking boots and used his mother's clothesline as a lifeline. Amazingly, no injuries were incurred from this neo-phyte outing and others like it. Wagstaff, a remarkable climber, has many first ascents on Calaveras Dome (northwest of Yosemite) as well as a first ascent in 1985 of the Celestial Peak in China during an expedition with Allen Steck and the American Alpine Club.

Steve Roper on Northeast Face of Cragmont, Berkeley

With the 1970s came a new breed of climber. Harder routes were led and difficult bouldering problems were popping up more frequently. Buildering, (climbing up or traversing around buildings) in the Bay Area became trendy, especially around many college campuses such as San Jose State and U.C. Berke-ley. Plenty of tickets were written by police and handed to the "crazy and extreme" climbers.

Jim McGowan, a former mountaineering instructor at the College of Marin, introduced many of his students and friends to rock climbing by taking them up to Mount Tamalpais in the 1970s. Among his students who contributed largely to climbing in the Bay Area were Tucker Tech, Everett Gordon, Maggie Pierce, and Eric Brand. Brand got hooked (or rather obsessed) and later became an accom plished big wall climber. In 1985, Brand used a mixture of aid, ice, and free climb-ing to snag a remarkable first ascent of the west face of Mount Thor on Baffin Island. Brand also has first ascents in Patagonia, Nepal, Pakistan, and Yosemite.

Long time Bay Area resident Russell Bobzien discovered and established a huge amount of bouldering at the Mickey's and Stinson Beach areas, as well as Turtle Rock (Ring Mountain) in the late 1970s. When Bobzien was bouldering in the North Bay in the late 1970s and early 1980s, John Sherman (famous for the "V" Vermin Bouldering Scale) was breaking new ground while bouldering at and near Indian Rock in the East Bay.

In the South Bay, Bruce Morris, John "Yabo" Yablonski, Marc Hill, Scott Cos-grove, Brad Watson, Jim Bridwell, Doug Robinson, David Caunt, Lee Orten-berger, and Bill Zauman were vital first ascentionists and uncompromising boulderers of the Castle Rock State Park and Skyline Boulevard climbing areas in the 1980s.

Topo Key

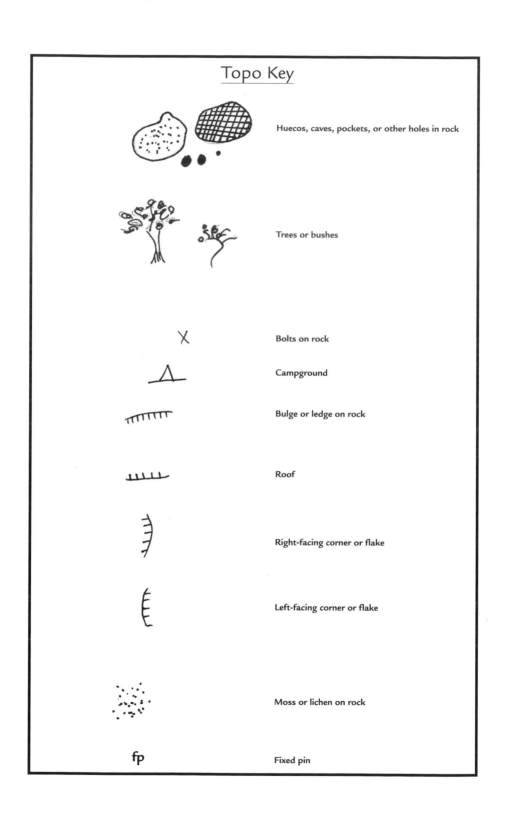

Huecos, caves, pockets, or other holes in rock

Trees or bushes

Bolts on rock

Campground

Bulge or ledge on rock

Roof

Right-facing corner or flake

Left-facing corner or flake

Moss or lichen on rock

Fixed pin

With "new fangled" equipment, such as cams, sticky rubber, and strong, solid bolts, there was a surge of route development in the 1980s. Climbers were testing their limits and difficulty ratings were rising. In 1990, buildering gave way to a more organized type of climbing with the birth of California's first indoor rock climbing gym, City Rock. Peter Mayfield (founder of Yosemite Guides as well as the aerial dance/climbing troupe Project Bandaloop) opened City Rock in Emeryville, which was the third climbing gym to open in the country. City Rock was the first to hold national climbing competitions, which dramatically escalated the interest and growth of rock climbing. Regardless of whether you are a gym rat, or an outdoor climber (who vows never to touch a plastic hold), the growth of indoor climbing was a catalyst to the explosion of rock climbing in the San Francisco Bay Area, opening the door to countless outdoor rock discoveries and ascents in the 1990s and into the new millennium.

How to Use This Book

The chapters in this book are arranged in order from the North Bay on down to the South Bay with the remaining crags that lie east of the Bay Area intermingled between these. Each chapter lists nearby amenities such as choice coffee houses, breweries, markets, and gas stations. Fees for parking are given, if they exist, and drinking water, rest rooms, and telephones in close proximity are listed. Camping facilities and dog restrictions (if any) are specified and described. Necessary information such as names of hospitals or emergency care facilities and directions are given, as well as average temperatures and the best season to visit each diverse climbing area.

Rating Systems for Technical Climbs

There are two types of ratings for the technical climbs in this guide: star (overall quality) ratings that range from no stars to five stars, and numerical (difficulty) ratings using the Yosemite Decimal System. Both are a matter of opinion and may differ greatly from one climber to another. I did my best to climb nearly every route listed in this guide. If a route was too difficult for me to even fall my way up, I tallied up several climbers' opinions on the difficulty and quality of the climb in question. If three separate climbers gave me completely different quality ratings of the route such as, "no stars," "three stars," and "five stars." I generally averaged it out, thus giving the route three stars in the guide.

If routes had bad anchors, crumbly or loose rock, funky bolt placement, or drilled pockets, I decreased the quality of the climb. Remember, just because a route has five stars does not assure you will love it. Conversely, you may find a one-star route a whole-lotta fun. It is speculative, and of course, relative. Some climbers live for technical, heart-pumping, runout slab climbing, while others prefer overhanging jugs with a bolt every five feet.

The Yosemite Decimal System is used in this book and throughout the San Francisco Bay Area. Although this system is relatively accurate, choosing a rating is subjective, so two climbs of the same rating may not have the same difficulty. The rating scale for technical climbs that require a rope currently begins at 5.0 and ends at 5.14. Above grade 5.10, the letters a, b, c, and d are used to further

V Scale converted to YDS (Yosemite Decimal System)

V0–	<5.9
V0	5.9–5.10b
V0+	5.10c
V1	5.10d–5.11a
V2	5.11a–5.11b
V3	5.11b–5.11c
V4	5.11d–5.12a
V5	5.12b–5.12c
V6	5.12d
V7	5.13a
V8	5.13b
V9	5.13c
V10	5.13d
V11	5.14a
V12	5.14b
V13	5.14c
V14	5.14d–5.15a

define the degree of difficulty. If you are new to outdoor climbing, be cautious of difficulty ratings. Don't get in over your head. Even if you feel comfortable leading 5.11s in the gym, chances are many outdoor 5.10s will scare the pants off you . . . if you even make it to the top. This is also true of climbers who are proficient in climbing at a particular venue. Just because you can scream up the overhanging pockets at Mount St. Helena, this does not mean you will be able to climb the same route difficulty on the bulgey, footless, sandstone slab at Castle Rock.

An R rating for runout means protection is sparse in at least one section of the route. Long falls are possible, with a heightened risk of injury.

An X-rated runout means a serious lack of protection. Either bad bolts, no bolts, or no good options for setting traditional protection means that falls from a route with this rating will mean serious injury or possible death for the climber.

Rating Systems for Bouldering

Bouldering difficulty ratings may (as a whole) be even more speculative and varied than climbing ratings. The Vermin Bouldering Scale (V Scale), developed by bouldering madman John Sherman, is unquestionably loose and should only serve as a guideline. The difficulty of a boulder problem does not take into account the potential for danger. For instance, if a problem 4 feet from the ground is labeled a V3, and another problem of the same difficulty tops out at 25 feet above jagged granite, the more dangerous problem is still labeled a V3 even though it undoubtedly takes much more skill (or folly). Highball boulder problems such as this are often labeled with an "R" (runout) after the numerical rating. Therefore, the above-mentioned problem may be labeled V3 R.

The huge popularity of bouldering is partially due to the social facet of the sport. Large groups of people often develop a camaraderie while working together on difficult problems, helping each other "crack the code" and accomplish complex moves. Conversely, some prefer the sport of bouldering because it can be performed without a belayer or the need for ropes, providing the opportunity for solitary escapes.

Chris Summit climbs Grotto Monkey, Cave Wall, The Grotto

North Bay Areas

MOUNT ST. HELENA

Mount St. Helena is a beautiful climbing destination inside the boundaries of Robert Louis Stevenson State Park. The peak of Mount St. Helena reaches 4,343 feet into the sky, overlooking Napa Valley vineyards and the famous town of Calistoga, with its mud baths, mineral spas, honeymooning couples, and strolling tourists. Grey foxes, coyote, and bobcats are known to roam the area. The uphill hike to the crag, though not overly difficult, deters enough people from climbing here, such that it is rare to see more than a handful of climbers on any given weekday. There are at least 55 different routes ranging from 5.6 to 5.12b. Most of these routes are bolted but some need additional protection to supplement long runouts.

Several worthy North Bay climbers have bolted and claimed first ascent on the majority of the routes. Sometime during the late 1960s and 1970s, Wade Mills and Forrest Shute cut the trail that leads from The Bubble to The Far Side, and soon after they bolted a 5.8 appropriately named Shute-Mills Route. Ken Stanton, Robin Madgewick, and Armin Fisher bolted several lines at The Far Side between 1988 and 1992. Mark Howe, Chris Summit, Jordie Morgan, Jason Campbell, and Jeff Follet discovered and bolted nearly all of the climbs at The Bear, The Bubble, and Crystal Pockets Area between 1990 and 1999.

Ross MacKenzie high above the vineyards on Jason and the Argonauts, *The Bear, Mount St. Helena*

Area Geology: Mount St. Helena geology is not only beautiful but also extremely rich in its abundance of color and form. The type of rock varies dramatically depending on its location on the mountain. The mountain itself, which is between 3 and 6 million years old, is part of the Sonoma Volcanics. The rocks were formed primarily by pyroclastic flows, much like those seen following the 1980 Mount St. Helens eruption in Washington State. "Pyro" (fire) and "clastic" (fragments and pieces) flows occur during violent eruptions, producing extremely hot ash, water, and mud, which then flows into layers, or "tuff." If the ash and mud is still extremely hot when it forms the layers of tuff, it becomes welded together, or "welded tuff." This makes great climbing material for the most part, such as that found in California's Owens River Gorge. But, tough exterior rock of this variety can also hide crumbly inner layers beneath the surface, so placing a bolt directly where you want it is not always possible. As a result, some lines on Mount St. Helena feature less than ideal bolt patterns and can be runout, particularly at The Far Side. Overall the climbing is marked by good pocket holds and huecos that require some attention to loose material typically near the top of certain climbs.

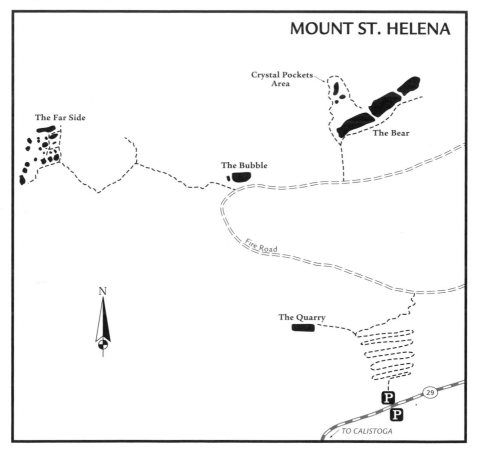

MOUNT ST. HELENA

Crystal Pockets Area

The Far Side

The Bear

The Bubble

Fire Road

N

The Quarry

P
P 29

TO CALISTOGA

TRIP INFORMATION

Climbing Season: The best time to climb here is from May to November. Wintertime and spring can offer good climbing, but it is often windy, and cold weather gear may be needed. It is not unusual to find beautiful days well into December. The lower section of The Bear provides excellent climbing if it is a hot day because the sun hits it in the morning, and usually by noon it is in the shade. The Bubble remains in the sun almost the entire day. Although The Far Side remains in the sun most of the day, this exposed western edge of the mountain can be buffeted by strong winds. The Quarry is sheltered and in the shade most of the day.

Fees: There are no current day-use fees for Robert Louis Stevenson State Park.

Camping: Camping is not allowed in Robert Louis Stevenson Park. The nearest campsites are located at the Napa County Fairgrounds. There are fifty sites available on a first-come, first-serve basis at a rate of $10 per night. The Fairgrounds are located at 1435 Oak Street in Calistoga. The phone is (707) 942-5111. Showers are available. Be sure to call ahead because campsites are not always available if festivals or car races are taking place.

Another camping option is Bothe State Park, located on California 29 between the town of St. Helena and Calistoga. The direct phone number is (707) 942-4575. There are fifty camp sites available plus a swimming pool, but reservations are required (for reservations call 800-444-7275). Campsites are $15, Sunday through Thursday; and $20, Friday and Saturday. Showers are available at 25 cents for three minutes. Weather and other park information is available on-line at www.cal-parks.ca.gov/counties/napa.htm.

Dogs: Dogs are not allowed inside the boundaries of Robert Louis Stevenson State Park.

Emergency Services: An emergency call box is located along CA 29, about 0.25 mile south of the Robert Louis Stevenson parking pullouts. The nearest medical facility, St. Helena Hospital and Health Center, is in the town of Deer Park, just south of Calistoga. It is open twenty-four hours and offers emergency care services. To get there from the crag, drive back down CA 29 southbound and veer left onto the Silverado Trail, just before the town of Calistoga. Drive south to the first traffic light, Deer Park Road. Turn left at Deer Park Road and continue for 0.25 mile where you will see the hospital signs directing you to your left. The phone number for the hospital is (707) 963-3611.

Water Sources: The closest source of water is in the town of Calistoga.

Telephones: The nearest pay phone is in Calistoga. For emergencies, use the call box on CA 29, about 0.25 mile south of the parking pullouts.

Restrooms: Unfortunately there are no restrooms at the park. Calistoga has public restrooms that are open during daylight hours. These are located at the community center next to the police station. From CA 29 westbound through town, turn right at the only traffic light onto Washington Street. Go one block. The sign for the public restrooms is on your left.

Father Mac counting his blessings on The Ladder, *The Bubble, Mount St. Helena*

Coffee Shops: A quaint little coffee shop with good java is on the main strip as you drive on CA 29 through Calistoga. Calistoga Roastery is on the north side of the road across from Calistoga Spas. It offers poached eggs, granola, pastries, and, of course, good coffee to get you geared up for the hike up the mountain to the crag. There are numerous cafes along the strip in Calistoga, but take into account that many are pricey due to Calistoga's robust tourism.

Markets: Cal Mart is also along CA 29 in Calistoga. It is on the north side of the road. Directly across the street is the Palisades Market, which has expensive but quality sandwich and snack items.

Brewpubs: The Middletown Brewery is on CA 29 at the bottom of the hill, northeast of the park. It should take you no more than 15 minutes to get there by car from the trailhead. The beer is good, but the food lacks the same quality.

Calistoga Inn offers microbrews on tap. Located on the corner of Lincoln and Cedar in Calistoga, the pub is a bit ominous with a comfortable, sultry, underground appearance.

Gas Stations: A Unocal and a Shell are across from one another on CA 29/Lincoln Avenue at the intersection of California 128/Foothill Boulevard.

Directions: From San Francisco, take U.S. Highway 101 northbound over the Golden Gate Bridge past Marin County and into Santa Rosa. Exit U.S. 101 at River Road/Guerneville and turn right onto Mark West Springs Road. Drive for 5 miles where Mark West will become Porter Creek Road. Drive another 4.5 miles and turn left onto Petrified Forest Road. Go 4.7 miles and turn right onto CA 128/Foothill Boulevard. Stay on CA 128 for 0.5 mile and turn left onto CA 29 at a three-way stop. CA 29 leads you through Calistoga. From the center of Calistoga on CA 29, drive 6.5 miles to where the hill crests. There is parking on both sides of the highway at the Robert Louis Stevenson State Park.

THE BUBBLE

The most frequented area at Mount St. Helena, The Bubble offers toproping and sport climbing on a chunk of volcanic tuff rising to 55 feet.

Approach: Getting there from the parking pullouts along CA 29 at the Robert Louis Stevenson State Park takes anywhere from twenty to thirty-five minutes depending on how fast you hoof it. Follow the trail on the north side of the road past the kiosk. Easy switchbacks head up for 0.75 mile to where a fire trail intersects. Here you will need to turn left and continue west up the dirt road for 0.5 mile to the rock formation at a large U-bend in the road. A third-class climb up a trail on the left side of the crag can access the toproping anchor bolts. Watch out for poison oak!

1. Face 5.7 ★★★ Toprope route. Short, but a good intro for beginners.

2. Solar Power 5.10c ★★★★ Four bolts to walk-off. This pockety route is fun and a little daring between the third and fourth bolts where a slight runout exists. There are two solid bolts waiting for you on top. Bolts are not suitable for rappelling. A walk-off to the west is necessary. Chris Summit, 1997.

The Bubble, West Face

The Bubble, South Face

3.   **5.10b ★★★** Four bolts to walk-off. Another fun route with lots of pocket options. Jordie Morgan, 1997.

4.   **The Ladder 5.9 ★★** Toprope route on overhanging buckets.

5.   **Bubble Boy 5.11b ★★★** Five bolts to chains. Very overhanging but juggy. The crux is a strange move over a small roof at the base. If starting left of the first bolt, skipping the crux, the route is rated at 5.10c. Jordie Morgan, 1997.

6.   **On the Road 5.10a ★** Toprope route

7.   **Catchy 5.11c ★★★** Eight bolts to chains. This is the longest route on The Bubble, with the crux consisting of an awkward move over a large bulge. Jordie Morgan, 1998.

8.   **5.10d ★★** Eight bolts to chains. This route veers to the right of *Catchy*, going up the chimney instead of climbing over the bulge. Long slings are needed to reduce horrid rope drag, and a nut or two are suggested to protect the base of the chimney.

THE BEAR

The Bear offers the best climbing at Mount St. Helena, but it comes at a price. The steep approach trail is definitely in need of improvement. Among the eighteen routes, there are three climbs that ascend a second pitch, beginning on a ledge.

Approach: Finding the rock can be difficult. From The Bubble, walk up the fire trail (east), for no more than 0.25 mile. Keep your eye out for a pine tree on the right edge of the trail. Its trailside branches are cut to allow clearance on the fire road, and it is close to 16 feet tall. You will find the crag directly across the fire road above the left side of the trail. There are noticeable sections of orange, white, and black. The trail isn't really a "trail," but more of a messy scramble straight up the hill for about 35 yards. This trail will lead you directly to the left side of The Bear.

1.   **Jeckyl & Hyde 5.10b R ★★★** Five bolts to cold shuts. Overhanging with good rests. A little runout at the top. Two guys from Angwen, 1998.

2.   **Rampage 5.10c ★★★★** Seven bolts to cold shuts shared with *Jeckyl & Hyde*. Pumpy and overhanging with big holds and huge feet. Sewn up! When you lower off you will realize how overhanging this section of The Bear is. Jeff Follet, 1998.

3.   **The Beast 5.11b ★★★★★** Four bolts to closed cold shuts. Great route that requires technical moves rather than big biceps. Heads up for the loose block above the crack!

4.   **The Beast 5.11b ★★★★★** Two bolts to closed cold shuts. Variation of *The Beast*. Need traditional gear to protect the crack for the first 20 feet. Pro to 3".

Ross MacKenzie on Kill Uncle, *The Bear, Mount St. Helena*

Mark Howe

The Bear, Mount St. Helena

5. **Jason and the Argonauts 5.12b ★★★★** Four bolts to closed cold shuts shared with *The Beast*. Certain "bomber-looking" holds are deceiving on this climb. Get agro! Jason Campbell, 1990s.

6. **Swallow My Pride 5.12b ★★★** Five bolts to cold shuts. Just plain hard. Jordie Morgan, 1990s.

7. **Kill Uncle 5.12a ★★★★★** Four bolts to cold shuts. A very "pretty" line. Pick your holds and move! Crux after third bolt. Jordie Morgan, 1990s.

7a. **Kill Uncle Direct Start 5.12a/b ★★★★★** Start directly under first bolt for a more difficult start.

8. **Arête 5.10b ★★★★** Four bolts to chains. A long sling is needed for the first bolt. Great fun. Crux near the second bolt. The crystals near the top are "purty," but they sure do smart!

9. **Mark's Moderate 5.10a R ★★** Four bolts on first pitch and five bolts on second pitch, to two-bolt anchor. The first pitch is a 5.9 chimney with an old piton between the first and second bolts. The second pitch is a dirty 5.10a with too much moss and lichen. Bring long slings for the bolts on the second pitch. Gear can be used to supplement bolts on the second pitch. There are chains (for *Theodore Roosevelt*) just up and left of the second pitch anchors that can be used for rappelling back down to the ledge, or you can walk-off the back and around *Crystal Pockets*. Mark Howe and Eric Berghold, 1999.

10. **Theodore Roosevelt 5.8 R ★** Four bolts to chain anchors. This climb can be supplemented with traditional gear in the runout section after the

THE BEAR

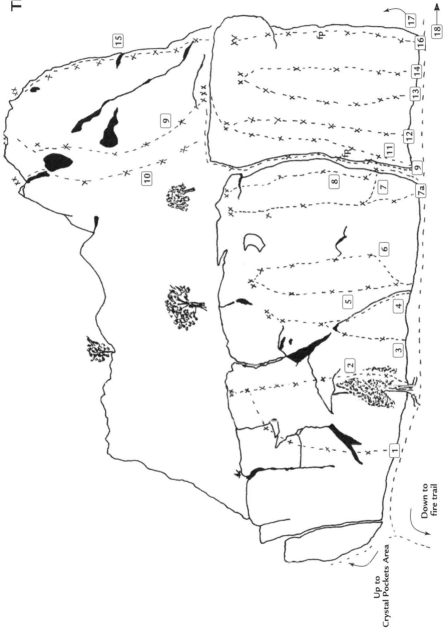

fourth bolt. Begins on the ledge above the first pitch of *Mark's Moderate*. Low angle climbing on rock with too much lichen. If lowering from chains to ledge, a 60-meter rope is necessary, otherwise the top of the climb will bring you above the eastern side of *Crystal Pockets* where you can walk down and to the left, bringing you back to the west side of The Bear. Mark Howe, 1999.

11.   **Black Hole Sun 5.10d** ★★★★★ Five bolts to rappell bolts. Check out the mono pockets, which are not necessary for ascension but fun to use. Another finesse line. Chris Summit, 1998.

12.   **Old and in the Way 5.11c** ★ Five bolts to rappell bolts shared with *Black Hole Sun*. One move wonder with the crux at the base. The rest of the climb is an uneventful 5.9. Jordie Morgan, 1990s.

13.   **Bears Choice 5.12a** ★★★ Six bolts to chains. Beta intensive start with interesting movement. Jordie Morgan, 1990s.

14.   **Napa Valley Party Service 5.11b** ★★ Four bolts to chains. Crux at base with easy climbing after the second bolt. Jason Campbell, 1990s.

15.   **Bear Arête 5.11a** ★★★★ Seven bolts to chain anchors shared with *The Bear* (5.9 crack). Starts at the far right end of the upper tier ledge. Leads up the right arête on the highest peak. Overhanging face climbing with the crux between the fourth and fifth bolt. Mark Howe, 1999.

16.   **Stone Free 5.11d** ★★★★ Five bolts to anchors with fixed biners for rappelling. Very strange technical route. Heads up! The roof after the third bolt is hollow in places. Crux between second and third bolts.

17.   **The Bear 5.9** ★★ Crack to chain anchors shared with *Bear Arête*. Pro to 4". To find this route, head east on the trail past *Stone Free* for about 30 feet. You will notice the crack in a corner, 20 feet in from the trail. Climb up 5.3 rock to the base of the crack. Belayer can tie into a tree for safety. Zigzagging crack with painful, sharp, angular holds. 105 feet!

18.   **Wayne's World 5.10c R** Seven bolts to anchors. Sketchy, crumbly rock. Good idea for belayer to wear a helmet. Head east on the trail past *Napa Valley Party Service* and *Stone Free*. Walk 20 yards until you notice a large right-facing flake that starts at the base of the wall and continues up and right for about 20 feet. Bolts are above the flake. Bring long slings. Eric Berghold, 1998.

CRYSTAL POCKETS AREA

There are four more climbs just above and left of The Bear in what is known as Crystal Pockets Area. *Pick Pocket* is a short 25-foot toprope with two solid bolts. The route (put up by Jeff Follet in 1998) goes at 5.10c, rather than 5.10b, due to the pain factor. The crystals in the rock are very sharp in certain pockets, and tape may be useful if losing skin is an issue.

Unknown climber, Bearclaw, *Crystal Pockets Area, Mount St. Helena*

The next route is also a toprope on a short wall to the right of *Pick Pocket*. This rock tops out at 35 feet. Jason Campbell placed bolts here, and the difficulty rating of the line is in question since nobody is known to have climbed it. It is dirty and partially covered in lichen.

Just up and right of the trail are the two bolted climbs, both much higher quality than the toprope routes. Both of the sport routes have rappel bolts, but you can walk off by carefully descending fourth-class material on the north edge of the rock.

Approach: Hike up third-class rocks and scree on the left side of The Bear until you see the bolts to your right (about 50 yards up). *Pick Pocket,* just to the right of the trail, is not very noticeable since the route is on the east side of the rock opposite the trail.

1.   **Crystal Pockets 5.10a ★★★** Route on left. Four bolts to two-bolt anchor. Start at a sawed-off tree stump and go up and left. A huge rest exists midway up the climb with a nice ledge to stand on and scope out the views. Chris Summit and Anu, 1997.

2.   **Bearclaw 5.11a ★★★★** Route on right. Six bolts to a two-bolt anchor. Beta intensive with many squared-off holds that are not as friendly as they look. Chris Summit, 1997.

THE FAR SIDE

Often referred to as Ganja Rocks, some may wonder whether a climber has smoked a little Ganja in order to trek all the way out here. Most routes here are easy to moderate. Bring traditional gear unless you can stomach long runouts.

Ken Stanton, Feelin' Your Oats, *The Far Side, Mount St. Helena*

Most lines have good pockets and cracks to place pro. Ken Stanton, Robin Madgewick, and Chris Summit put up the majority of these routes between 1989 and 1999. Stanton and Madgewick intended the routes to be largely traditional climbs with a few bolts here and there, but since then others have placed more bolts on many of the routes, making them a mixture of traditional and sport.

Approach: Facing The Bubble, the trail begins immediately left past a tree and a clump of bushes. The trail winds west, crosses above an outcropping of loose rock, which is not The Far Side. Keep hiking over the saddle through a narrow trail with a series of rises and short descents. A fork in the trail is taken on the left, which will lead you down the mountain, and then up again to the base of The Far Side. A long, 55-foot-tall, bolted route stands directly in front of you (see *Shute-Mills Route* on the overview diagram). Good luck! A trail skirts the perimeter of the formation and branches off between rocks.

1. **Seymour Frishberg 5.9 R ★★★** Three bolts to two-bolt anchor. South-facing arête on the farthest west developed formation at The Far Side. Robin Madgewick and Ken Stanton, 1990.

THE FAR SIDE

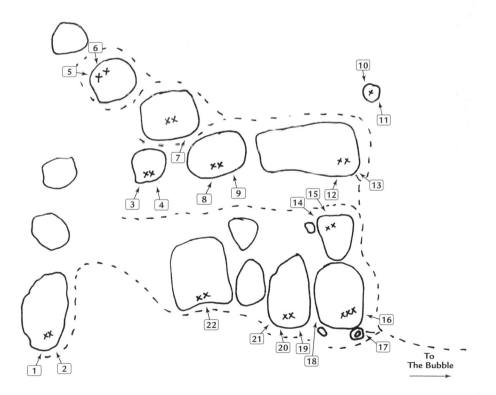

2.   **Boneless Chicken Ranch 5.11b ★★★** Four bolts to two-bolt anchor. East-facing route that heads up and to the right. Robin Madgewick and Ken Stanton, 1990.

3.   **5.8 ★★★★** Two bolts to two-bolt anchor. Chris Summit, 1999.

4.   **5.8 ★★★** Two bolts to two-bolt anchor. Chris Summit, 1998.

5.   **5.10a ★★** Two bolts to walk-off.

6.   **5.11d ★★** Two bolts to walk-off.

7.   **Kola 5.9 ★★★★★** Four bolts to two-bolt anchor. Chris Summit, 1999.

8.   **Atlas 5.10b ★★★** Two bolts to chains. Robin Madgewick and Ken Stanton, 1990.

9.   **Atlas Shrugged 5.10a ★★** Two bolts to chains. Ken Stanton and Curtis Crawford, 1991.

10. **North Crack of Hummingbird Spire 5.7 R ★** An anchor bolt is set for toproping.

11. **South Face of Hummingbird Spire 5.9 ★** An anchor bolt is available for toproping.

12. **5.8 ★★** Toprope route.

13. **5.10 ★★** Toprope route.

14. **War Party 5.11b R ★** Two bolts to two-bolt anchor. Jeff Follet and Chris Summit, 1993.

15. **The Chief 5.10c ★★★★** Three bolts to two-bolt anchor shared with *War Party*. Jeff Follet and Chris Summit, 1993.

16. **Shute-Mills Route 5.8 ★★★★★** Five bolts to three-bolt anchor. This was the first climb to be bolted at The Far Side. Wade Mills and Forrest Shute cut a trail from The Bubble and used 0.25-inch bolts with home-made hangars. In 1993, Jeff Follet and Chris Summit re-bolted the climb, and Ken Stanton fittingly named it the *Shute-Mills Route*.

17. **The Pile 5.9 ★★** Pro to 2″. Short traditional climb, which can be linked up into *Shute-Mills* at the third bolt extending the ride. This route was named after the nearly disastrous bowel distress of Robin Madgewick during the first ascent. Robin Madgewick and Ken Stanton, 1990.

18. **Saviour Heart 5.9 R ★★★** Three bolts to three-bolt anchor. Ken Stanton and Robin Madgewick, 1990.

19. **5.9 ★★★** Four bolts to two-bolt anchor. Jeff Follet, 1993.

20. **Better Eat Your Wheaties 5.10d R ★★★** Four bolts to two-bolt anchor. Ken Stanton and Robin Madgewick, 1991.

21. **Feelin' Your Oats 5.10a R ★★★** Three bolts to two-bolt anchor. Armin Fisher and Robin Madgewick, 1988.

22.   **Step to the Left 5.8 R ★★** Two bolts to a two-bolt anchor. Don't use third bolt, which is to the right, due to a large loose block. Robin Madgewick and Armin Fisher, 1988.

THE QUARRY

This is a toprope and traditional climbing area with routes up to 75 feet. There is only one bolt on the face of the rock. There is a two-bolt chain anchor on top of the face, but due to its extremely old and rusty appearance, it is wise to anchor the top with webbing over the precipice using the chains as backups. You can get to the top by carefully ascending the third class, eastern edge of the formation. Two right-facing cracks make for fun traditional climbing.

The ratings here range from 5.6 to a 5.10c. The 5.10c leads straight up past the only bolt. A long traverse across the face in several crack systems make this an excellent area to practice traditional placements incorporated with lead climbing.

Approach: The Quarry is the closest developed climbing formation to the trailhead. From the parking lot, hike east past the kiosk up the switchbacks. In about 0.5 mile you will see a clearing where the Robert Louis Stevenson cabin once stood. There is a stone book—a monument of the site—on the right side of the trail. Hike left and up a gully from the site for about 50 yards, where you will see The Quarry. There is an old mining shaft at the western end.

Russell Bobzien on Fort Ross Boulders

FORT ROSS BOULDERS

Fort Ross is the northern-most area detailed in this guide. The inclusion of Fort Ross marks its impeccably clean sandstone and airy, dynamic bouldering problems. Although some North Bay climbers preferred to keep the Fort Ross jewel a bit of a secret, over the past several years more and more boulderers from other parts of the Bay Area have taken the time to travel to this area, which has roughly only a third of the number of problems that Sunset Boulders (a.k.a. Goat Rock) has to offer.

In the spring of 1996 Cazadero climber and resident Richie Esquibel was searching for new rock to conquer and spotted the boulders from California 1. When Esquibel first viewed the boulders up close he didn't realize the full potential of the sandstone. He left the area thinking that there may be a couple decent problems but nothing of exceptional quality. Within a couple weeks he returned to the cove to re-assess the boulders' potential and found many classic lines, ranging from V4 through V8. Word spread quickly, and within months, the Fort Ross Boulders were getting chalked up by climbers from Sonoma County and beyond.

Most landings at Fort Ross are exceptionally protected by soft flat sand (there are a few boulder problems on the beach, farther south from the main rock, that are directly above huge jagged edges of rock). Long dynamic moves are required on some sections of the nearly featureless, "slope-arific" sandstone which, depending on tide and sand levels, reaches more than 20 feet in height. The other boulders are scattered about the small cove, less than 0.5 mile end to end.

Fort Ross was a colony composed of Russians and Alaskan natives between the years of 1812 and 1841. This colony bought several hundred acres of the land from the Meteni Indians for a more-than-reasonable sum of three blankets, three pairs of pants, two axes, three hoes, and a few beads. Nowadays if you could find that much land for sale along the coast, you might have to hawk your climbing gear and come up with an additional 50 million or so. The fort was well armed and vigilantly manned by the Russians. After the colony severely over hunted the local sea otter population, they turned to agriculture and stock raising as new occupations. The agricultural efforts failed, and in 1841 the property was sold to John Sutter of Sutter's Fort in the Sacramento Valley. The name "Ross" is short for "Rossiya," the Russia of Tsarist days.

Only three of the most popular boulder problems will be included here. For a more comprehensive guide to Fort Ross bouldering problems, see *The Wine Country Rocks* by Chris Summit, a climbing and bouldering guide to Sonoma and Mendocino counties.

Area Geology: When you are bouldering at Fort Ross, you are moving, even when you are standing still, albeit at less than a snail's pace. The boulders sit on the Pacific side of the San Andreas fault, which moves northward an average of 5 centimeters each year. The boulders are a mix of bedded and massive sandstone, which has not been metamorphosed. Mother Nature threw in a small amount of granite to spice things up.

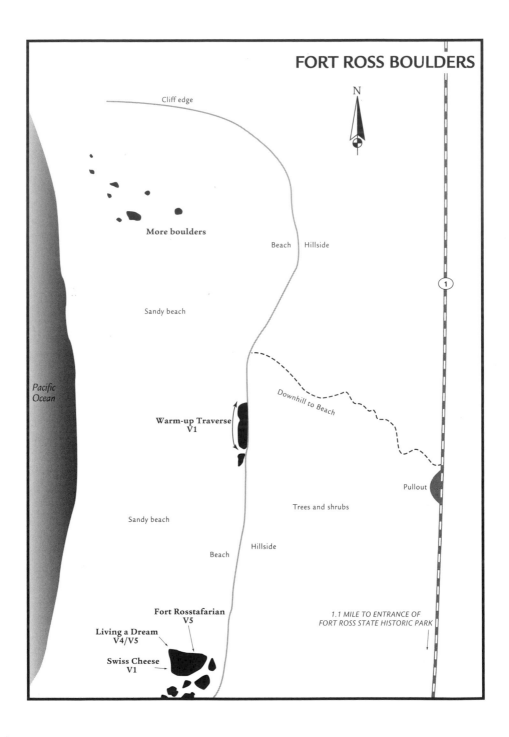

FORT ROSS BOULDERS

N

Cliff edge

More boulders

Beach   Hillside

Sandy beach

Pacific
Ocean

Downhill to Beach

Warm-up Traverse
V1

1

Pullout

Trees and shrubs

Sandy beach

Hillside

Beach

Fort Rosstafarian
V5

*1.1 MILE TO ENTRANCE OF
FORT ROSS STATE HISTORIC PARK*

Living a Dream
V4/V5

Swiss Cheese
V1

Russell Bobzien

Jason Hicks rips it up at Fort Ross Boulders

TRIP INFORMATION

For details on this area, see the Trip Information under Dry Creek Sea Crag. These areas are just a few miles apart.

Directions: Follow the directions from San Francisco to Jenner under the section for Dry Creek Sea Crag. From the intersection of CA 1 and California 116 in Jenner, the Fort Ross State Historic Park is 11 miles north on CA 1. From the entrance to the park, drive exactly 1.1 miles north on CA 1 to a pullout on the west side of the road. For further directions to CA 1 along the coast, see directions in the section Dry Creek Sea Crag.

1.   **Living A Dream V4/V5** This starts on the northwestern arête of the main rock. Standing in front of the arête, go up the left side, following the curve to the top section of rock.

2.   **Fort Rosstafarian V5** Begins at the base of the north side of the rock in the center and requires long moves on small edges up the face and over the top.

3.   **Swiss Cheese V1** Starts on the right of the west side of the main rock. Go a little to your left and then straight up.

Chris Summit on Judge Dredd, *Main Wall, Dry Creek Sea Crag*

DRY CREEK SEA CRAG

It is a shame that more climbers do not take advantage of this pristine climbing destination. The steep hike, which takes fifteen to twenty-five minutes in and twenty to thirty minutes on the way out (if you know where you are going), ensures solitude and beauty, not to mention extremely satisfying climbing and bouldering.

Although this area is known for its difficult sport routes, climbers will find a half dozen fun moderate lines as well. You can even Tyrolean traverse using the farthest rock to the west, known as Galapagos, and the large boulder on the east side of it. The three-bolt climb on Galapagos goes at 5.10a. There are also bolts on top of Galapagos, as well as a piton. In addition, a boulder just east of Galapagos Boulder features two bolts on the top for the Tyrolean.

Dry Creek was developed in the 1980s by Mark Howe and Dave Melrose. Although most climbers are unaware of it, there is also good bouldering here. For bouldering problems and ratings check out *The Wine Country Rocks*, written and self-published by Chris Summit.

Area Geology: A mixed basket of eggs along the California Coast usually means that the area is a fault zone. Dry Creek is in one such zone. The crag has mainly Franciscan blue schist in a massive form. When a rock was originally massive it was literally cooked, and as a result, deformed so that none of the original structure is left. There is also some bedded chert at Dry Creek, which has not been metamorphosed (changed from its original structure).

TRIP INFORMATION

Climbing Season: It gets a bit chilly along the Sonoma County coastline. Be prepared for thick fog and/or cloud cover, as well as temperatures often 10 to 15 degrees cooler than in San Francisco. When the wind picks up, T-shirt weather can change rapidly to down jacket weather. Fall is usually the prime time to climb here, but with the wacky coastal weather, perfect days are also common in the winter months.

Fees: There are no fees for the Vista Trail parking lot at the Sonoma Coast State Beach.

Camping: Fort Ross Reef, 7 miles north on California 1, has twenty campsites available on a non-reservation system for $12 a night. The sites are in a wind-protected canyon just south of the fort. Drinking water and toilets are available but not showers. The campsites are only available between April 1 and November 30. Camping is also available in Jenner at the Pomo Indian Campsites. See the section on Pomo Indian Boulders.

Dogs: There are no posted restrictions regarding dogs at Dry Creek Sea Crag.

Emergency Services: The nearest hospital is Kaiser in Santa Rosa. This is 26 miles from Jenner. The hospital is located at 401 Bicentennial Way; the phone number is (707) 571-4000. The alternate hospital is also in Santa Rosa. Santa

Rosa Memorial is located at 1165 Montgomery Drive; the phone number is (707) 546–3210.

Water Sources: There are no fountains or other water sources near the parking lot or the crag. Jenner is the closest area you will find water.

Telephones: Unfortunately, if you need to use a phone, you are out of luck unless you head south back into Jenner. Driving north, the closest phone is at Fort Ross State Historic Park.

Restrooms: There is an outhouse at the corner of the parking lot where the trail to the crag begins.

Coffee Shops: There are no coffee shops in the town of Jenner. The closest coffee joint is in the quaint little town of Duncans Mills, 9.7 miles from the crag. Gold Coast Coffee Co. is on Moscow Road, just off of California 116, and 3.6 miles east of the junction of CA 116 and CA 1.

Markets: The Fast and Easy Mart is the only sort of market in Jenner. It is at 10438 California 1. Duncans Mills offers a general store on CA 116 at B Street. From the junction of CA 116 and CA 1 south of Jenner, head east on CA 116 for 3.5 miles and look for Duncans Mills General Store on your left side.

Brewpubs: Not only does Duncans Mills offer a coffee shop and a market, but it also is home to a great little pub called The Blue Heron. A fine selection of beer is available, as well as a full bar and a menu, with everything from nachos to oysters. To find The Blue Heron, drive east on CA 116 (from its junction with CA 1) for 3.6 miles and turn right onto Moscow Road. The Blue Heron will be on your right, next to the post office.

Gas Stations: The closest gas station is in Jenner, 6 miles south of Dry Creek Sea Crag, on CA 1.

Directions: From San Francisco, head north on U.S. Highway 101 over the Golden Gate Bridge. Continue through Marin County and into Petaluma. Exit at East Washington, turn left, and drive back over the freeway. Stay on this road, which will take you through downtown Petaluma, then continue west. Note: The road will turn into Bodega Avenue, and after 26 miles, the road becomes CA 1 (northbound) in Bodega Bay. Drive north on CA 1, passing CA 116 in Jenner. From this junction, continue north for 6.1 miles to the Sonoma Coast State Beach and the Vista Trail parking lot on your left.

From Santa Rosa, the quickest route to the crag is via CA 116. Drive westward until you get to the CA 1. Turn right and follow CA 1 for 6.1 miles to the Sonoma Coast State Beach and the Vista Trail parking lot on your left.

Approach: Head northwest to the trail at the corner of the parking lot next to the outhouse. Keep hiking north on the trail, crossing over an old fence and continuing left and downhill toward the sea. If you pass a large boulder mass sitting alone in the middle of a field, you have gone too far north and should go back and find the trail heading west. The trail meanders a bit along a ridge and finally splits left and right. Head right to access the main area of the crag. This will also lead directly to the bolts above the routes.

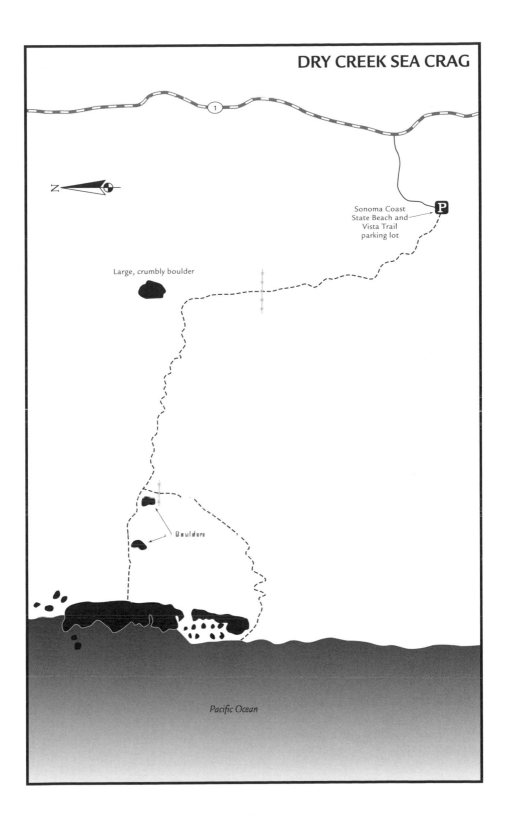

DRY CREEK SEA CRAG

N

Sonoma Coast
State Beach and
Vista Trail
parking lot

P

Large, crumbly boulder

Boulders

Pacific Ocean

Sucka Fish *and* The Sea Cave *routes, Dry Creek Sea Crag*

1.   **Sucka Fish 5.12a ★★★** Three bolts to chain anchor. Stick-clip first bolt, or climb *The Sea Cave* and clip bolt on the way down. Bouldery crux off the ground. Chris Summit, 2000.

2.   **The Sea Cave 5.10c ★★★** Three bolts to chain anchor shared with Sucka Fish. Jason Campbell, first ascent on toprope. Bolted by Chris Summit, 1999.

3.   **Rackless Crack 5.10d ★★★★★** Three bolts to rusty cold shuts. Nice crack with some sharp edges. Greg Miller, first ascent, 1992. Reluctantly bolted by Chris Summit and Jeff Follet, 1996.

4.   **Bohemian Bypass 5.12b/c ★★** Mixed traditional gear for the crack at the start plus nine bolts to a three-bolt anchor. Major rope drag. Long slings needed. Mark Howe, 1993.

Main Wall, Dry Creek Sea Crag

Mark Howe, first ascent of Pseudo Bohemic Hitchhiking Youth, *Dry Creek Sea Crag*

Mark Howe

5. **Pseudo Bohemic Hitchhiking Youth 5.12d** ★★★★ Eight bolts to a three-bolt anchor. A hold recently broke between the fifth and sixth bolts making the route a bit harder. Mark Howe, John Grush, and Dave Melrose, 1992. Bolted on lead in 1996.

6. **Judge Dredd 5.13b** ★★★★★ Nine bolts to three-bolt anchor. Travels up and left. Requires dynamic moves on tiny, tricky holds. Chris Summit, 1997.

7. **Jury Duty 5.13c** ★★ Nine bolts to three-bolt anchor. Follows first five bolts of Judge Dredd, then traverses right and finally up the top of *The Sandbagger*. Unfortunately, there is a drilled pocket on the route. Also known as *The Fundamentalist*. Dave Melrose, 1992. Later bolted by Jim Thornburg and Jason Campbell.

8. **The Sandbagger 5.7** ★★★ Crack pro to 2". Very short route that psyches you out! Committing first move. Mark Howe, 1992.

9. **The Interesting Block 5.6** ★★ Pro to 4". This corner requires frequent mantling. Climb up fourth-class junk to get to the base of the climb.

10. **Sport Wall Face 5.11a** ★★★★★ Three bolts to two-bolt anchor. Cruise up fourth-class rock to the base of the climb. Protect the horizontal crack before the first bolt. Skirt right and up to the first bolt, then continue upward, finding the nice edges and moving past the crux after the second bolt, to the top. Strip draws when lowering, except anchor draws, which can be retrieved from reaching over the edge on the summit. Mark Howe, 1990.

11. **Crack 5.8** ★ Pro to 2". Head up and left, reaching up over a dihedral, then pulling over to a thin finger crack.

12. **Crack 5.9** ★★★ Pro to 2". Take the ride on the crack going up the center of this wall. Good warm-up. The crux is pulling the short roof with a finger to hand crack above it.

13. **Crack 5.7** ★★ Pro to 3". Easy low angle face climbing leads to a fist crack with nice features for feet.

14. **Crack 5.6** ★ Pro to 2". Face climbing to short thin crack on the right side of the wall.

15. **Crack of Zorro 5.10b** ★ Pro to 1". To the left of *The Sport Wall Face*. Can share anchors with *Sport Wall Face*, but get ready for a big swing if you come off! Scary, not-so-safe lead. Dave Melrose, 1992.

16. **Red Wall Face 5.10a** ★★★★ Three bolts to two-bolt anchor. The 5.10a move is just past the first bolt, then the ride slows down, although it does go up. Bolted by Chris Summit, 1999.

17. **Little Roof 5.10d** ★★ Short and sharp toprope! Get your feet up high and go! Mark Howe, 1991.

Sport Wall, Dry Creek Sea Crag

Crack Wall, Dry Creek Sea Crag

Red Wall, Dry Creek Sea Crag

Galapagos, Dry Creek Sea Crag

18. **Galapagos 5.9 ★★★★** Three bolts to two-bolt anchor. This climb is extremely dependent on tide and weather. Must be done at low tide in the summer and autumn months. Off-shore weather in winter and early spring can cause larger waves to visit the rocks; so although you may be ready to climb on a bright sunny day at low tide, your belayer may not be quite as willing to brave the splashes of cold Pacific water. Step from a boulder across water to begin, then go up, passing three bolts. Bolts are on top of the rock, but they are not rappel bolts. Take a leaver-biner or webbing. The one at the eastern edge enables you to Tyrolean traverse back to shore, using a piton on the boulder east of Galapagos Boulder—notable highlight at Dry Creek. Bolted on lead by hand by Mark Howe, 1996.

Richie Esquibel on Ohaus, V5, Pomo Indian Boulders

POMO INDIAN BOULDERS

Pomo Indian Boulders is secluded, pristine, and above all, peaceful. Surrounded by clover and towering redwood trees, these boulders are the perfect escape from city life. There are only a few problems here, but the few that are here are fine indeed. The boulders lie inside the boundaries of the Pomo Indian Campground and are gated off between December 1 and March 31. Accessing the boulders during these months requires a short walk for 0.5 mile from the dirt road to the campground.

Currently there are only a dozen developed problems at Pomo Indian Boulders. Eight of these are on the largest boulder, fittingly called Pomo Rock. The side of the rock opposite the campsites and parking lot holds the majority of the problems. A cave with bomber underclings and slippery slopers provides most of the fun. The problems range from V0 to V6. Almost all have high scary top-outs with very bad landings onto potentially painful rocks in and around the stream. Crash pads and spotters are recommended. Two 10-foot boulders are in the center of the creek only a few feet downstream of Pomo Rock. These sport a V0 and an overhanging V2. Another boulder, southeast of Pomo Rock, also has a couple of fun problems. A few quality problems on Pomo Rock are listed in this section.

For a complete guide to this area, pick up a copy of *The Wine Country Rocks* written by Chris Summit and available at Shoreline Mountain Products in San Rafael, California.

Area Geology: The main 45-foot rock at Pomo Indian Boulders is comprised mainly of Franciscan serpentinite. Serpentinite, the state rock of California, consists almost wholly of minerals in the serpentine group: antigorite, chrysotile, and/or lizardite. This rock is formed from the alteration of seafloor peridotite—the mantle material that is underneath the earth's crust—at high pressures and fairly low temperatures. At roughly 140 million years old, this is a relatively old rock. Serpentinite is usually white, green, yellowish green, or mottled green and gray, much like the main rock at Pomo Indian Boulders.

TRIP INFORMATION

For additional information on the area, see Sunset Boulders. You will find a description of the climbing season along the north coast, as well as listings for emergency services and amenities. Pomo Indian Boulders is about 4 miles from Sunset Boulders.

Fees: The day-use parking fee (which was recently $2.00) has been axed. It is now free to park here during the daylight hours.

Camping: You do not need to travel far for camping. There are twenty-one sites available here from April 1 to November 30. No showers are available. The sites are $7.00 per night on a first-come, first-serve basis.

Dogs: Dogs are not allowed at or near Pomo Indian Boulders or the campground.

Water Sources: Drinking water is available near the parking lot at the campground.

POMO INDIAN BOULDERS

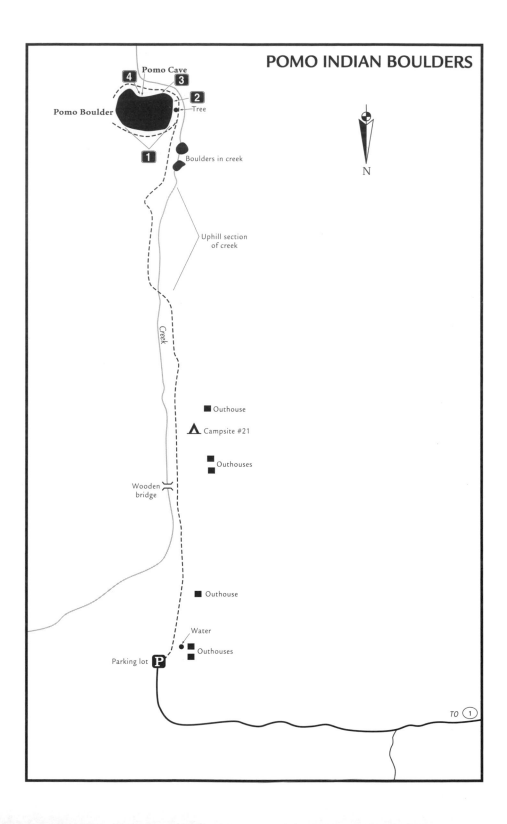

Pomo Cave

4 **3**

2

Pomo Boulder — Tree

1

Boulders in creek

N

Uphill section
of creek

Creek

■ Outhouse

▲ Campsite #21

■ Outhouses
■

Wooden
bridge

■ Outhouse

Water
● ■
■ Outhouses
■

Parking lot **P**

TO ①

Telephones: There are no phones at the Pomo Indian Campground. The closest one is in Jenner, 1 mile north on California 1 from the intersection with Willow Creek Road.

Directions: Travel to Jenner from San Francisco following the directions under Sunset Boulders. Then drive north of the sign for Goat Rock State Beach on CA 1 for 0.5 mile. Turn right on Willow Creek Road at the Sizzling Tandoor restaurant. Drive 2.8 miles on the paved road and turn right on the dirt road that leads to the Pomo Canyon Trailhead. Drive 0.5 mile to the end of the dirt road into the parking lot.

Approach: Take the trail that leads left past the outhouses at the corner of the parking lot. Follow a small creek past a wooden bridge. Continue walking with the creek on your left until it heads uphill and the trail becomes faint. Cross the creek here and follow it up past several large boulders that lie in the middle of the creek. You cannot miss the 45-foot Pomo Rock on the edge of the creek.

1. **Pomosapien Traverse V4** There is a large tree up against Pomo Rock next to the creek. Facing the rock, start the traverse on the left side of the tree and head left around a cruxy corner and uphill.

2. **Chalupa V1** Begins right of the tree and left of the arête. Sit-start on good edges that make way for jugs up and over the top. This top-out is not as scary as the boulder problems leading over the cave area.

3. **Ohaus V5** Begin inside left edge of cave and climb out and up the upper half of the arête to the top.

4. **Pomo Roof V2** Start low underneath the cave and climb straight up and over the roof.

Ted Danigelis on Hard On Traverse, *Sunset Boulders*

SUNSET BOULDERS (A.K.A. GOAT ROCK)

The Sunset Boulders are located in a field above Goat Rock State Beach off California 1, south of Jenner. These boulders are undoubtedly the most popular climbing destination in the North Bay. Easy accessibility, pristine beauty of the coastline, cool climate, and fine boulder problems are the primary reasons for the area's popularity. The Sunset Boulders are frequently used for youth day camps and for instructing adults on toproping and beginning climbing techniques. For more information on bouldering at The Sunset Boulders, see *The Wine Country Rocks*, written and self-published by Chris Summit.

Area Geology: The Sunset Boulders are green and blue schist. If schist is green, rather than blue, it means it had a lower metamorphism; it did not descend far into the earth where it would have been subject to greater forces and heat. These rocks in particular have a high "schistosity," meaning they have been pulled apart like taffy in a fault zone. The schistosity is the "flakiness" of the rock, like a pie crust. Garnets are also present in the rock. Climbers familiar with this area claim that as late as the 1980s garnets used to be scattered on the ground below all the rocks.

TRIP INFORMATION

Climbing Season: Although temperatures along the north coast tend toward chilly, the cooler conditions are often a blessing in the summer when other climbing locations in the Bay Area can get warm enough to require chalking up as frequently as grabbing holds. If lingering fog is not an issue, the area offers nearly perfect conditions often even in the dead of winter. With the coastal winds wicking away the moisture within a few hours, the rock dries fairly quickly after a rain. Annual rainfall averages 44 inches, mostly during the winter months. Temperatures here in the summer will rarely reach 80 degrees. In the winter, temperatures during the day rarely rise above 60 degrees, so climbing with hot cocoa breaks is common.

Fees: There are no fees for climbing or parking at The Sunset Boulders.

Camping: There are fabulous camping spots very close to the boulders. The Bodega Dunes Campground is 7.1 miles south of Goat Rock State Beach, off of CA 1. There are ninety-eight sites available at $12 a night on a first-come, first-serve basis. Showers are available. There are also great campsites at Doran Park at the south end of Bodega Bay. More than eighty-four sites exist at $16 a night. From The Sunset Boulders, drive south on CA 1 past Bodega Bay and turn right on Doran Park Road. Follow the signs to the campsites. Reservations are needed here (707–565–2041).

Dogs: There are no restrictions regarding dogs at the Sunset Boulders, but dogs are not allowed at Goat Rock State Beach.

Emergency Services: The nearest hospital is Kaiser in Santa Rosa. This is 26 miles from Jenner. The hospital is located at 401 Bicentennial Way. The phone number is (707) 571-4000. The alternate hospital is 2 miles farther. Santa Rosa

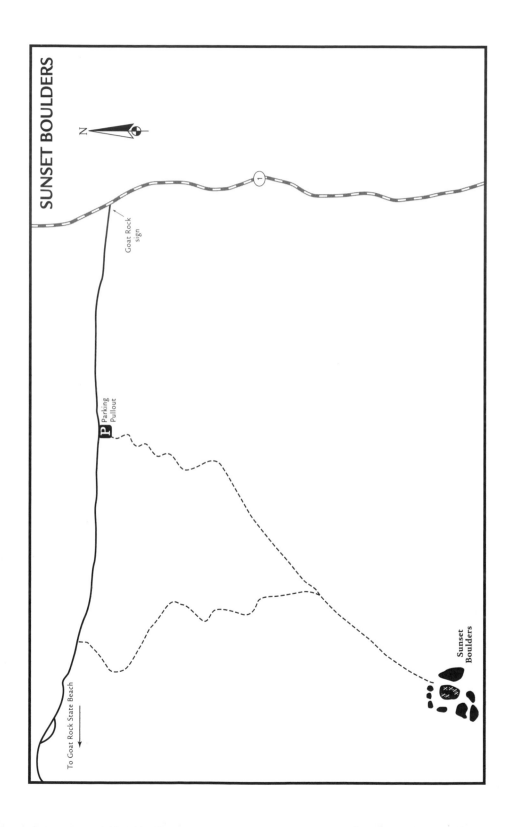

SUNSET BOULDERS

N

Goat Rock
sign

1

P Parking
Pullout

To Goat Rock State Beach

Sunset
Boulders

Lynn Cuthbertson on Sunset Face, *Sunset Boulders*

Memorial is located at 1165 Montgomery Drive. The phone number is (707) 546-3210.

Water Sources: There is a water fountain down at Goat Rock State Beach at the end of the road near the restrooms. From the parking pullout that leads to The Sunset Boulders, you will need to follow the road for 1.5 miles to Goat Rock State Beach.

Telephones: A pay phone is located on a dirt road next to the restrooms at the beach parking lot.

Restrooms: To find the restrooms at Goat Rock State Beach, drive past the boulders down to the beach. The restrooms are along the east side of the parking lot.

Coffee Shops: Roadhouse Coffee Co. is located 15 miles south of Jenner at 2001 North CA 1 in Bodega Bay. It is open 7.00 A.M. to 3:00 P.M., daily and has all the basics—coffee, espresso, and pastries.

Markets: There are no supermarkets nearby, but you should be able to find most items at Diekmann's Deli and Market on the west side of CA 1 at Taylor Street in Bodega Bay.

Brewpubs: If traveling along California 116 toward Santa Rosa, after leaving the boulders, you will find a great little pub called the Blue Heron in Duncan Mills. A fine selection of beer is available, as well as a full bar and a full menu, with everything from nachos to oysters.

Gas Stations: The closest place to fill up is the Texaco in Bodega Bay on CA 1, less than 1 mile north of the junction with Bodega Avenue. It is next door to the Sonoma Coast Tourism Center.

Directions: From San Francisco, take U.S. Highway 101 (northbound) through Marin County and into Petaluma. Exit the freeway at East Washington/Central Petaluma and turn left, driving over the freeway. East Washington goes through downtown Petaluma and becomes Bodega Avenue. Stay on Bodega Avenue. From this point, drive 26 miles on Bodega Avenue/Valley Ford in a westerly direction. Bodega Avenue/Valley Ford will become CA 1 (northbound) when you reach Bodega Bay. Drive 9 miles, where you will notice a sign on your left directing you to Goat Rock State Beach. Turn left and drive 0.25 mile to the parking pullout on the left side. The boulders will be visible in the large grassy fields below you.

SUNSET BOULDERS

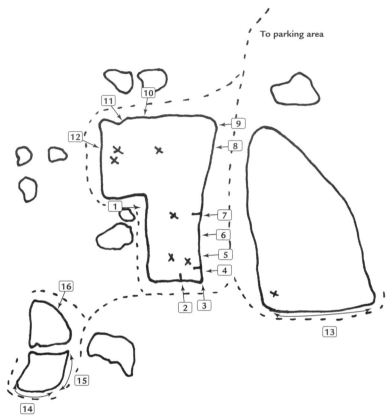

1. **Approach 5.2 ★** The easiest way to get above to set up topropes.

2. **Crack 5.9 ★★**

3. **Arête 5.8 ★★★★**

4. **Pelican Crack 5.10a ★★★** Don't use the arête to the left.

5. **Sea Breeze 5.11c ★★★** No fair using cracks to the left and to the right. Very small edges and balance will take you to the top.

6. **P.M. 5.10c ★★★★** Crack to face.

7. **Killer Crack 5.10c ★★★** Face moves proceed this off-finger crack.

8. **Face 5.5** Another hike up to set ropes.

9. **Off the Wall 5.8 ★** There are a couple of 5.8 moves, but the rest of the route is easier.

Sunset Boulders, also known as Goat Rock

10. **Face 5.8** ★★

11. **Corner 5.7** ★ Stem up on good edges and fine handholds.

12. **Sunset Face 5.9** ★★

13. **Sunset Traverse V1** ★★★★ Long traverse. Great warm-up!

14. **Hard On Traverse V4** ★★★★ Traverse from right to left, using a funky cross and dynamic lunge midway through the problem

15. **Hard Right V3/V4** ★★★ Stay low on this overhanging traverse from left to right.

16. **The Specialist V5** ★★★★ Very popular problem that begins with a sit-start pulls through a flake, and goes over a lip.

RING MOUNTAIN

Ring Mountain in Marin County is one of the most frequented bouldering and climbing spots in the North Bay. The mountain features something for nearly everyone at every level. Split Rock has toprope routes ranging from 5.3 to 5.8 on the face and lines that go at 5.11 inside the split. The highest section of rock reaches nearly 25 feet. Turtle Rock offers exceptional bouldering with moderate to difficult problems, as well as a very popular V4 traverse.

Long-time Marin resident Russell Bobzien discovered and pioneered Turtle Rock in 1977, when he was only nineteen years old. He quickly brought his older brother Gary Bobzien out to Ring Mountain to check it out. The Bobzien brothers cleared a dense patch of poison oak from the large overhanging section of rock. The elder Bobzien got the worst of it, enduring raw seeping skin for days. The name Turtle Rock was actually derived from a boulder a few hundred yards to the south, but unfortunately it was surrounded by a subdivision and remains behind a closed gate. Since the original boulder at Turtle Rock became off limits, the Bobzien brothers started calling their new boulder Turtle Rock, and the name stuck. A small boulder on top of the formation looks like a turtle from a certain angle.

Sharp angular holds and slick feet characterize most of the bouldering problems. The landings are fairly good on most sections of the rock, which reaches 15 feet at its highest point. When the air is clear, the views are amazing. Split Rock overlooks the East Bay and the Richmond-San Rafael Bridge, while Turtle Rock, standing higher on the hill, gives a great view of the skyscrapers in downtown San Francisco, as well as Mount Tamalpais.

Area Geology: Ring Mountain was actually a very popular place in the 1890s. Many rare minerals and other exotic rock types were discovered on the northern crest of the Tiburon Peninsula, prompting visits from geologists from all over the globe. All of the different minerals and rock forms found here have since been discovered in different parts of the world, but it is still widely known that the strange mixture and varieties that exist together here have not been found together in any other area on earth.

The mineral Lawsonite was discovered here. It was discovered on a formation (just south of Turtle Rock in the hills of Bel Aire above Tiburon) that was destroyed by blasting and bulldozing in 1964 in order to build homes. Lawsonite indicated that metamorphism (recrystallization of the rock) had occurred under conditions of great pressures but at very low temperatures.

Rocks here had their origin as sediments deposited approximately 100 million years ago. Submarine volcanic activity accompanied the sedimentation, resulting in basalt flows, which in turn accounts for the layering effect found on much of the rock. The underlying rock mélange below Turtle is thought to extend several hundred feet below the earth's surface, though this is still only a theory.

Various unusual weather-resistant types of rock are spattered across the hillside. Such rock masses are a mixture of several different Franciscan rocks and

Jason Scharp on Turtle Rock at Ring Mountain, with the San Francisco skyline in the background

minerals: serpentine, greywacke, shale, chert, pillow lava, gabbro, rodingite, harzburgite, different types of schists, and jadeite, just to name a few.

In addition to the rare rock forms, the very first petroglyphs seen in the Bay Area by archeologists were discovered on Ring Mountain. All of the petroglyphs were carved in similar chlorite schist. A large boulder down the hill on the southwest side of Turtle Rock has petroglyphs on it. Be careful not to tread (or smear) on the glyphs!

TRIP INFORMATION

Climbing Season: It can get very windy here. Bring a sweater or jacket as a precaution even in the summer months. Weather patterns in the North Bay have been changing over the last couple of decades. Summers seem to start later, with the rainy season often extending into May. Indian Summers are common, making September and October filled with warm, sunny, and dry days. Hot temperatures in summertime can make many slick problems on Turtle very greasy. The average high temperature here in the summer is 80 degrees.

Fees: There are no fees at Ring Mountain. It is designated as an open space preserve.

Camping: China Camp State Park, east of San Rafael, is the closest campsite to Ring Mountain. From Taylor, drive back down and turn left onto Paradise Drive. Continue north and proceed onto U.S. Highway 101 (northbound). Drive less than 3 miles and exit at Central San Rafael. Make your first right onto Second Street, which will turn into Point San Pedro Road. Continue east and around the peninsula on San Pedro Road. China Camp State Park will be on your left. Campsite fees range from $12 to $16. The phone number is (415) 546-0766.

Dogs: There are no restrictions on dogs, or any other beast, at Ring Mountain.

RING MOUNTAIN

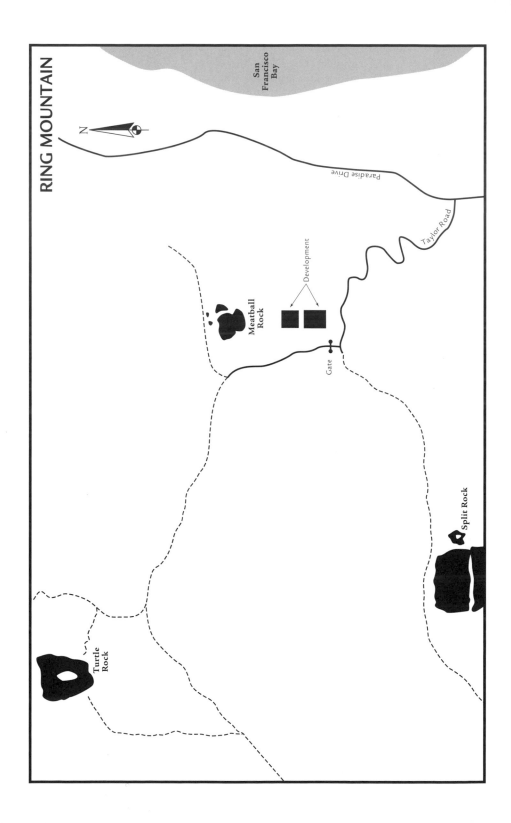

San Francisco Bay

Paradise Drive

Taylor Road

Development

Gate

Meatball Rock

Turtle Rock

Split Rock

N

Emergency Services: California Highway Patrol (CHP) offices are located along Paradise Drive near U.S. 101. The nearest emergency facility is the Urgent Care Center, located on the southwest side of U.S. 101 and Paradise Drive. The center is not open twenty-four hours.

The nearest hospital is Marin General at 250 Bon Air Road in Greenbrae. To get there from Ring Mountain, drive back down Taylor Road. Turn left on Paradise Drive and continue onto U.S. 101 (northbound). Exit at Sir Francis Drake Boulevard, less than 2 miles north, and head left (west). Go 1 mile and turn left on Bon Air Road. The hospital is 200 yards ahead on your left. The direct phone number to the hospital is (415) 925-7000.

Water Sources: There are no fountains or other sources of water on Ring Mountain. The closest water would be at a liquor store on Paradise Drive next to World Gym. This is between San Clemente Drive and Seawolf/El Camino Drive.

Telephones: Pay phones are located at the little shopping center on Paradise Drive near the liquor store and World Gym.

Restrooms: Unfortunately, the closest restroom is at the mall inside Macy's next to U.S. 101 and Paradise Drive. Good luck trying to get the guys at the liquor store to let you use theirs. They are sticklers. There is a 76 gas station on the west side of U.S. 101.

Coffee Shops: There is a coffee stand outside of Nordstroms at the Village Mall next to U.S. 101. The coffee is decent but nothing to get too excited about. From Ring Mountain, drive back down Taylor Road and turn left onto Paradise Drive. Instead of turning left, which leads you onto U.S. 101, turn right onto Redwood Highway. The mall will be on your left.

Markets: On the other side of the freeway (west side), you will find the Town Center, which has several eateries and a Safeway. To get there, head west on Tamalpais Drive/Paradise Drive from U.S. 101 and make your first right onto Madera Boulevard. Safeway is on your right.

Brewpubs: Marin Brewing Company is the closest brewpub to the site. The pub features good beer and grub. In the back, there is a nice outdoor patio with heaters available for chilly nights. Sometimes it gets a little crowded. If you visit on $2.00 Tuesdays, it may appear as if you have entered a frat house. But once again, the beer is good, as well as the food. It is located at Larkspur Landing, across from the Larkspur Ferry Terminal. From Paradise Drive and U.S. 101 head north, exit at Sir Francis Drake, and turn right. Make your first left at Larkspur Landing Circle. Turn right into the large parking lot where you will notice the brewpub left of a fitness center.

Gas Stations: There is a 76 gas station on the west side of U.S. 101 on Paradise Drive/Tamalpais Drive.

Directions: From San Francisco, take U.S. 101 (northbound) over the Golden Gate Bridge into Marin County. Go 6 miles and exit at Paradise Drive/Tamalpais Drive in Corte Madera. Turn right off the freeway, then right again on San Clemente. After 2 long blocks, the road becomes Paradise Drive. Continue straight for 3 miles, passing a school on your left. Turn right onto Taylor Road, continue up until the road ends, and park here.

Split Rock, Ring Mountain

SPLIT ROCK

Countless North Bay residents have learned how to set up a toprope here. A good-sized tree and several cracks on the top offer many options. Easy access to the top of the rock is gained on the back (south) side. Split Rock is where the local climbing gym and various youth groups often bring first-timers for an outdoor climbing experience. A nice hand-to-fist crack on the main face can be climbed and traditionally protected. Various lines on the main face go at 5.3 to 5.8. More difficult climbing is inside of the split; a 2-foot-wide chimney section is often top-roped.

SPLIT ROCK, INSIDE

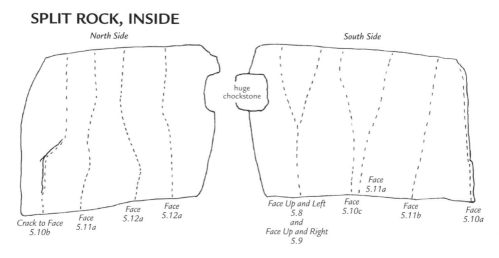

Turtle Rock at Ring Mountain on a busy summer day

TURTLE ROCK

Some folks choose to set up a toprope on Turtle Rock depending on the height and difficulty of the problem. The highest point on the rock is 20 feet. You will find everything under the sun here—slick slopers, funky mantles, sharp crimps, and an abundance of greasy footholds. Landings are generally good, but a crash pad may provide that extra margin of safety. A 40-foot traverse goes at V4.

MEATBALL ROCK

This smaller rock, which reaches less than 20 feet, can be toproped. Lines on the north face range from easy 5.6 to 5.10 on an overhanging section. Watch out for glass at the base of the rock. In 2001, a large home was built within 10 yards of Meatball Rock, so the fate of the rock is unknown.

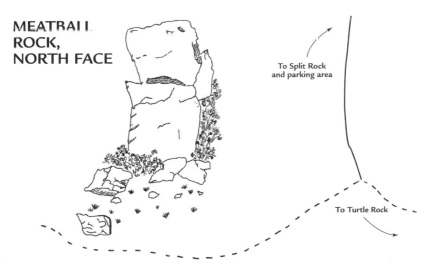

MEATBALL
ROCK,
NORTH FACE

To Split Rock
and parking area

To Turtle Rock

Rich Galagaran, Oberman's Crack, *Mount Tamalpais*

Ron Capasso

MOUNT TAMALPAIS

Mount Tamalpais, the birthplace of mountain biking, is a must for beginner climbers. Known locally as "Mount Tam," this 2,571-foot peak offers fun climbing with fantastic views of San Francisco, the East Bay, and the stellar Pacific Coast. On a very clear day, such as one following a rain and wind, depth perception is enhanced remarkably. Mount Diablo, some 30 miles to the east, Mount St. Helena, some 60 miles to the northeast, and the Farallon Islands, 25 miles out to sea, look as if they are just a few miles away.

Miwok Indians lived here for countless generations before Europeans arrived. Most students of American Indian lore and the Miwok tribe believe the name "Tamalpais" means West or Coast Mountain. The outline of the eastern edge of the peak is said to resemble a sleeping woman. This is why Mount Tam is often referred to as the "Sleeping Maiden."

In the mid-1800s, trails were constructed, as well as a railway to the top of the mountain, known as the "Crookedest Railroad in the World." A wildfire damaged the rail line in 1930 and it was put to rest. You will notice the old rail ties near the foot trail that leads from the parking lot to the lookout point on the peak. Wildlife is abundant, with various species of birds, deer, rabbits, bobcats, and even mountain lions and wild boars calling Mount Tam home.

Climbing here ranges from 5.3 to 5.11b. Most of the climbing is toproping, but some routes can be traditionally led, and the cracks and pockets make a great place for aspiring trad leaders to practice setting protection and building anchors. Approaches and belay areas are very safe and comfortable, but because the climbing crags jut out around the top of the peak, climbers will appreciate the illusion of being much higher than they actually are.

Mount Tamalpais is in a state park, which is open from 7:00 A.M. to sunset every day of the year. Occasionally the park is closed if there is serious fire danger. It is wise to call ahead during the summer months (415-388-2070).

Area Geology. The rock here is comprised mainly of the mineral serpentine. The mountain marks the site of a former subduction zone, due to the fact that it was ocean crust, which had been hydrothermally altered. Serpentinization is the process of removing all calcium from rocks, replacing it with magnesium. The serpentinization occurred when the rock was ocean crust. Hot water percolated through the crust altering it into the formation, which now stands. Very few plants can live in soil without calcium, besides chapparal (pines and manzanita), which cover a good portion of the mountain. Serpentine is the state rock of California.

Trip Information

Climbing Season: When it is cold and foggy at the beach crags, chances are it is warm and sunny on Mount Tam. The peak is often above the fog band that envelopes the coast, the city, and southern Marin. Autumn is the best time to climb here for mild temperatures and fair weather, but if no rain is in the forecast, climbing at Mount Tam is possible year-round. Sun hits the North Formation and The Leaning Tower in the morning and early afternoon. Shade can be found on the Southern Formation and on Oberman's Rock most of the day.

Fees: Day-use parking fees are $2.00.

Camping: There are several great places to camp near Mount Tam. Pantoll Campground is the closest. It has sixteen campsites operated on a first-come, first-serve basis. RVs are allowed but on a limited basis. The campground is located at 801 Panoramic Highway. There are no showers, but running water is available. From the top of Mount Tam, drive down East Ridgecrest Boulevard and turn left on Pantoll Road. The sites are at the intersection of Pantoll Highway and Panoramic Highway. For information, call (415) 388-2070.

Dogs: Leashed dogs are allowed on the main trail that leads up to the summit rocks. Certain trails nearby do not allow dogs at all. These have postings at the trailheads.

Emergency Services: A pay phone is located in front of the restrooms east of the parking lot. The nearest hospital is Marin General, which is at 250 Bon Air Road in Greenbrae. To get there from Mount Tam, backtrack to U.S. Highway 101 and head north. Exit at Sir Francis Drake Boulevard and head left (west). Go about 1 mile and turn left on Bon Air Road. The hospital is 200 yards ahead on your left. The direct phone number to the hospital is (415) 925-7000.

An alternate facility is Marin Urgent Care, located at 101 Casa Buena Drive in Corte Madera. This center has limited hours and you should call ahead if help is required on weekends or evenings (415-925-4525).

Water Sources: Water fountains are located near the restrooms at the park. During some of the winter months, the water for the fountains is shut off. If this is the case, the sinks in the bathrooms always have constant flow, but it is difficult to fit a water bottle underneath them so come prepared.

Telephones: A pay phone is in front of the women's restroom. If it is not working properly, the next closest one is at the Pantoll Ranger Station, down the road at the intersection of Pantoll Road and Panoramic Highway.

Restrooms: The park does a great job of keeping the restrooms very clean. They are located just east of the parking lot.

Coffee Shops: Many locals visit Peet's Coffee in downtown Mill Valley before heading to the top of Mount Tam. It is located at 88 Throckmorton Avenue in the heart of downtown Mill Valley. From U.S. 101, exit at Stinson Beach/CA Highway 1, continue west from the freeway. Go straight through the first intersection, which becomes Almonte Boulevard. Almonte shortly becomes Miller Avenue, which will lead you straight into downtown Mill Valley and the intersection of Throckmorton Avenue. Peet's is easily recognizable by the line of eclectic individuals often trailing out the front door. If the line is too long, or strong coffee is not a priority, there are two other coffee shops on the same block.

Markets: Just off of Shoreline Boulevard in Mill Valley, on the way to Mount Tam, you will find Bell Market. The deli is open during daylight hours. Exit at

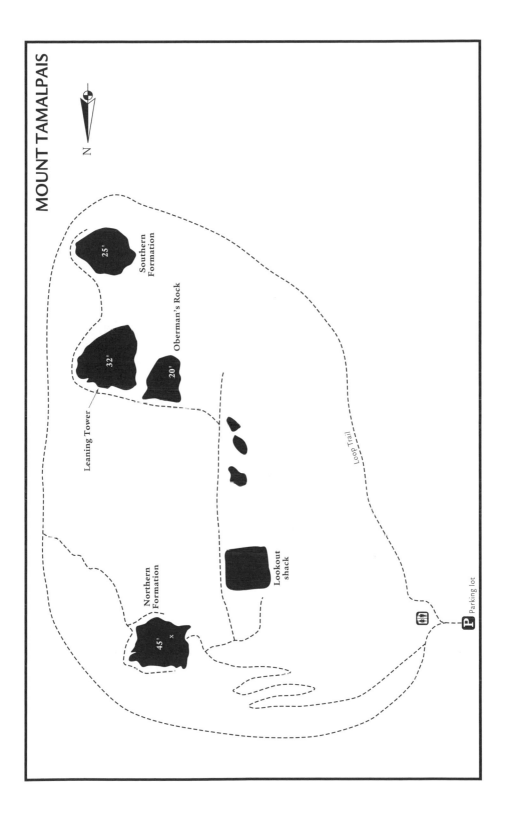

MOUNT TAMALPAIS

N

Southern
Formation
25'

Oberman's Rock
20'

Leaning Tower
32'

Northern
Formation
45'
x

Lookout
shack

Loop Trail

Parking lot

the Stinson Beach/CA 1 exit and drive west on Shoreline Boulevard to the first traffic light. This is known as Tam Junction. Turn left here continuing on Shoreline. Make a left at the first street, Flamingo Road. The store is on your left, across from Chevron.

Brewpubs: The Pelican Inn at Muir Beach offers Bass, Guiness, spirits, darts, and great atmosphere. The inn is located just off CA 1 at Muir Beach Road. From the top of Mount Tam, drive down Panoramic Highway, and instead of turning left onto Shoreline Boulevard, (which leads back to U.S. 101), turn right onto Shoreline and continue less than 3 miles down toward Muir Beach. The pub will be on your left.

Gas Stations: There is an ARCO on the corner of Shoreline Boulevard and Almonte Boulevard. There is also a Chevron on Shoreline at Flamingo Road in Mill Valley.

Directions: From San Francisco take U.S. 101 (northbound) over the Golden Gate Bridge into Marin County. Exit at Stinson Beach/CA 1. Head west on Shoreline Boulevard (CA 1). Turn left at the second light, continuing on Shoreline. This is known as Tam Junction. Drive up Shoreline until you come to a distinct fork in the road. Turn right here onto Panoramic Highway, following the signs to Mount Tamalpais. Continue on Panoramic until you come to Pantoll Road, where you will need to turn right. Make the next right onto East Ridgecrest Boulevard, which will lead you directly into the parking lot.

NORTHERN FORMATION

The Northern Formation offers fun toproping with routes ranging from 5.4 to 5.8. It tops out at 50 feet. The northern lines generally increase in difficulty for the most part, from the northwest around to the eastern arête on the rock face. An abundance of cracks and slingable chocks make setting up topropes here easy. Approach from the western side, where the main trail leads. The east face has toprope routes ranging from 5.5 to 5.8

1.   Face 5.4 ★★
2.   Face 5.6 ★★★
3.   Arête 5.8 ★★★★
4.   Face 5.7 ★★
5.   Face 5.7 ★★

Melinda Heard on the Northern Formation, Mount Tamalpais

Northern Formation, Mount Tamalpais

Oberman's Rock, Mount Tamalpais

OBERMAN'S ROCK

This 20-foot roof offers the only 5.11 climbs at Mount Tam. Essentially two routes exist. The prominent overhanging *Oberman's Crack* can be either traditionally led or toproped. A line can also be climbed that follows the left side of the crack using only the holds on the face.

6.   Oberman's Crack 5.11b ★★★★

7.   Face 5.11b ★★★

LEANING TOWER

This 40-foot rock has moderate toproping routes ranging from 5.3 to 5.10d. See photo on page 66.

8.   Face 5.5 ★★

9.   Face 5.10b ★★★★★

10.   Arête 5.8 ★★★★

11.   Old Bolt Line 5.10d/11a ★★ Only old rusty, hangerless bolts remain on this slick section of rock. Using your right hand on the arête, climb over the slippery section of wall to the top. Poor feet.

12.   Face 5.5 ★★★

13.   Face 5.3 ★

SOUTHERN FORMATION

Although only about 30 feet in height, the southernmost rock is great for setting protection and learning how to lead climb. A 5.7 line begins with two parallel cracks at the base. See photo on page 67.

14.   Crack to Face 5.7 ★★★★

Leaning Tower, Mount Tamalpais

Southern Formation, Mount Tamalpais

Kenny Ariza on Naked and Disfigured, *Main Rock, Mickey's Beach*

MICKEY'S BEACH

Mickey's Beach is the most rapidly changing crag in the Bay Area due to its location—smack dab on the edge of the Pacific Ocean, with many routes often partially covered in water. Erosion and significant rock and boulder movement take place annually. Tides and sand levels at the base of many rocks change dramatically from day to day. Many routes can only be climbed at low tide, and checking a tide table is recommended before making plans.

The tide can come in very quickly and with huge amounts of force, causing danger for climbers, as well as belayers. For a web link to tide predictions at Mickey's, see the section on climbing season. Routes at Mickey's that are tide dependent are noted in the route descriptions. In addition to the variance of the physical appearance of the rock, the variance of the condition dependent rock is quite drastic, meaning the surfaces can range from tacky and graspable to downright slick. Heavy fog is also a significant factor in daily climbing conditions. Despite these caveats, Mickey's is a Bay Area favorite.

Many routes have been re-bolted in recent years. Currently most bolts appear and feel solid with the exception of a pair of rusty old cold shuts used as the anchor for *Hot Tuna*.

The largest rock, known as Main Rock, had a huge portion break off and fall into the sea in 1993. Unfortunately four very popular climbs went along with it. Twenty-two climbs (plus a few variations) currently exist on the Main Rock, which houses a total of more than 130 bolts. If you notice lonely bolts or anchors without any bolts leading to them, chances are these bolts are remnants of previous climbs that broke off into the ocean.

The climbs now on Main Rock range in difficulty from 5.10b to 5.13b. There are two U bolts on the southwest edge of the top of Main Rock. These can be used to rappel down to various anchor bolts to set up the topropes. Use caution when rappelling from the top due to loose rock that can potentially fall on people below. There are two smaller formations with bolted routes next to Main Rock. Grey Slab and Peeper Rock house three routes from 5.9 to 5.10a.

Less than a mile south on the beach from the Main Rock is The Egg (previously referred to in older guides as "Whales Back"). The eight routes here range from 5.6 to 5.12c.

Behind, and a tad south, of The Egg is a lonely rock known as California Slab. Most of the rock is slabby, but a large wall on the west side has a nice wide roof crack. This rock is not climbed much anymore and the crack is said to be very dirty. The longer slab routes up the left side are moderate, ranging from 5.7 to 5.9.

Even farther south of The Egg and California Slab is Endless Bummer Rock, which only has two routes, but both are quality lines. One bolted route is 5.13; the other, 5.14. This area is not exactly popular due to the intense difficulty of both routes.

In addition, there are numerous great boulders along the Stinson Beach and Red Rock Beach. Many boulders continually shift in the sand with the tides and water levels, causing changes in the angles, lengths, and often the difficulty of problems. (Note: Do not be surprised if you see lots of naked people running around playing Frisbee and building rock cairns. Red Rock is generally a nude beach.)

Area Geology: The variance of rocks and formations at Mickey's and Stinson lead geologists to believe that the beaches lie on a strand of the San Andreas fault zone that has crumbled and mixed up the myriad of rocks we now see there. Large amounts of breccia (pronounced 'brech-ee-ah') is in the area. Breccia can be any type of rock that has been ground up and has angular fragments. It is often produced in faults.

Most of the climbing and bouldering rocks are meta-greywacke. A greywacke is a fine-grained sandstone with quartz, feldspar, and various dark rock grains that are cemented into a fine-grained matrix. Endless Bummer Rock has most of these mentioned materials in it but a much higher concentration of sandstone. Swiss cheese-like pockets known as tafoni appear on Endless Bummer's over-hanging face.

The rocks (before the present formations) were actually sediments deposited off the coast and brought down on the Farallon plate as it subducted (or slid beneath) the North American plate.

TRIP INFORMATION

Climbing Season: Of all the areas in this guide, Mickey's is by far the most "condition dependent" crag. Heavy fog, crashing waves, and weird coastal weather patterns can make or break a good day at Mickey's. The rock generally dries quickly here since it is often windy. Autumn is usually the best season. If the tide is out, or not an issue, there is no fog, and the rock is dry, climb on!

For daily weather information, call (415) 868-1922. Unfortunately, the recorded message on this line does not always mention whether or not fog is present. For daily tide predictions on-line, see www.co-ops.nos.noaa.gov/tides/westSF.html.

Fees: No fees are required at Mickey's, Red Rock, or Stinson.

Camping: Steep Ravine Campground and Cabins is the closest campground to the climbing areas. In fact, if you are climbing at The Egg, the campground and cabins are only a short stroll away. There are six tent sites and ten cabins, which can sleep up to six people each. The campsites range from $7.00 to $11.00, while the cabins are $30.00. Showers are available at 50 cents for five minutes. Reservations are required usually months in advance unless you come during the week when there are often first-come, first-served sites available. Call (415) 388-2070 weekdays between 9:00 A.M. and 5:00 P.M.

Dogs: Stinson Beach Parks Department does not allow dogs on any of the beaches.

Emergency Services: The Stinson Beach Fire Department is on California Highway 1, about 50 yards north of the intersection of Arenal Avenue and less than 1 mile north of the large parking lot that leads down to Main Rock.

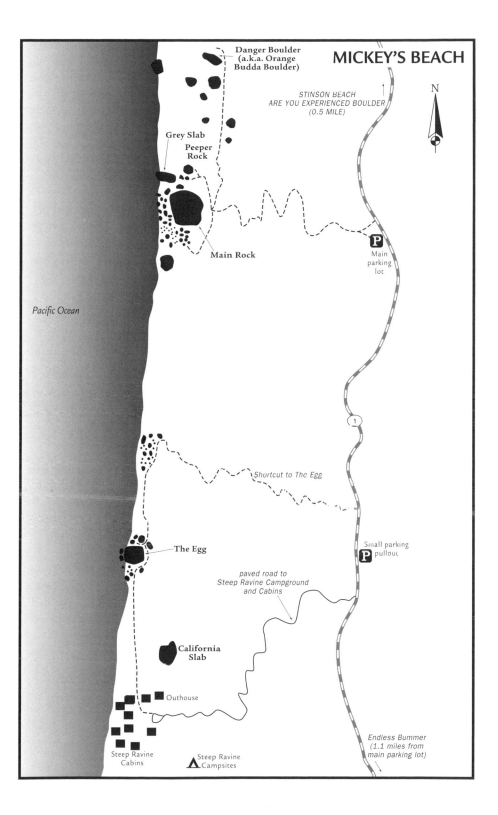

MICKEY'S BEACH

N

Danger Boulder
(a.k.a. Orange
Budda Boulder)

STINSON BEACH
ARE YOU EXPERIENCED BOULDER
(0.5 MILE)

Grey Slab
Peeper
Rock

Main Rock

Pacific Ocean

Main
parking
lot

1

Shortcut to The Egg

The Egg

Small parking
pullout

paved road to
Steep Ravine Campground
and Cabins

California
Slab

Outhouse

Endless Bummer
(1.1 miles from
main parking lot)

Steep Ravine
Cabins

Steep Ravine
Campsites

The nearest hospital with emergency services is Marin General in Greenbrae. It is 15 miles away. Drive back on Shoreline Highway toward Mill Valley and U.S. Highway 101. Hop onto U.S. 101 (northbound) and drive 4.4 miles, and exit at Sir Francis Drake exit in Larkspur. Take the off-ramp west toward Fairfax and Greenbrae. Continue west on Sir Francis Drake for 1.3 miles and turn left onto Bon Air Road. After 1 block, locate the hospital on the left side of the road.

Water Sources: Steep Ravine Campgrounds and Cabins has drinking water. At the base of the stairs next to Main Rock, there is a pipe that provides water from a natural spring. Drink at your own risk. There are also drinking fountains near the main beaches at Stinson.

Telephones: The closest pay phones are near Stinson Beach. There is a phone at the edge of the walkway between the parking lot at Stinson Beach and the Parkside Café on Arenal Avenue, off Shoreline. There is another pay phone in front of Beckers' Groceries, on the north side of Shoreline at Calle Del Mar.

Restrooms: There is an outhouse at the Steep Ravine Cabins and restrooms at Stinson Beach.

Coffee Shops: The tastiest coffee at Stinson is at the Parkside Café. This cute little joint is located on Arenal Avenue off Shoreline Highway.

Markets: Beckers' Groceries has a fine selection of deli items, including sandwiches, sodas, and Cheetos. It is on the north side of Shoreline across the street from the road that leads into the main parking lot for Stinson Beach (not Mickey's).

Brewpubs: On the drive back toward U.S. 101, following Shoreline/CA 1, you will pass Muir Beach, where a fine little pub exists. The Pelican Inn, on the west side of Shoreline, has an ample selection of beer on tap, as well as wine by the glass. Food is available, but it is a little pricey.

Gas Stations: An ARCO and a Chevron are next to one another on Shoreline just 1 mile west of U.S. 101.

Directions: From San Francisco, take U.S. 101 (northbound) over the Golden Gate Bridge into Marin County. Exit at CA 1/Stinson Beach. Head west on Shoreline/CA 1. Turn left at the second light, continuing on Shoreline. This intersection is known as Tam Junction. Stay on Shoreline/CA 1, following signs to Stinson Beach. You will come upon a fork in the road where you can continue straight ahead or veer right onto Panoramic Highway. Continue straight ahead, following the signs for Muir Beach and Stinson Beach. From the fork, you will need to drive 7.6 miles to get to the large parking lot, which leads to Main Rock and the other areas at Mickey's Beach. The parking lot is 0.3 mile north of the road that leads to the Steep Ravine Campground and Cabins.

MAIN ROCK

Routes 10 through 22 are tide dependent.

Approach: To reach Main Rock, take the prominent trail at the west side of the large main parking lot that winds down to the water. Main Rock is at the end of the dirt trail. The trail can lead you directly to the top of the rock, or you can follow paths to the left or right to reach the bolted routes below.

East Face

1. **Unknown 5.11c R ★★★** Three bolts to a two-bolt anchor. This route is more-or-less a one-move wonder, but a fun one. The first bolt is 20 feet off the deck, reached by relatively easy 5.9–5.10a moves. The third bolt is a serious reach, then tackle the 5.11c move just below the anchors, where two tiny crimpers are all you have to work with.

2. **Corner Route 5.10b R ★★** Two bolts to a three-bolt anchor. This route, which is over 45 feet, only has two bolts. Toproping it is an option.

3. **Walk a Thin Line 5.10c R ★★★★★** Five bolts to a three-bolt anchor. Take your bifocals. The holds up top are pretty tiny. The bolt a few feet below and right of the anchors is not actually on route, but because of the runout section near the top, many people choose to clip it anyway. This route has been known to scare the bejeezus out of many climbers. Eric Brand, 1984. Bolted by Tony Yaniro, 1985.

4. **Pelicans 5.12a ★★** Six bolts to a two-bolt anchor. Very reachy, footless bulge between the third and fourth bolts. Easier climbing after fourth bolt.

5. **Holy Mackerel 5.13a ★★★★** Seven bolts to a two-bolt anchor. A combination of dynamic moves and power will lead you past the crux (between the third and fourth bolts) on to the top. Russell Bobzien with first toprope ascent, 1983. Bolted by Marcos Nunez, 1996.

Chris Summit

Richie Esquibel on Sex Porpoises, Main Rock

6. **Wet Dreams 5.12c/d ★★★★** Eight bolts to shared two-bolt anchor with *Dreams of White Porsches.* Russell Bobzien with first toprope ascent, 1983. Marcos Nunez bolted, 1996.

7. **Dreams of White Porsches 5.13b ★★★** Seven bolts to two-bolt anchor shared with *Wet Dreams.* Russell Bobzien first toprope ascent 1983.

8. **Dream On 5.13b ★** Seven bolts to two-bolt anchor. Shares first four bolts with *Dreams of White Porsches,* then heads right into *Insomnia.* Some bolts are rusty on this line and word has it that an important hold broke recently, increasing the difficulty.

9. **Insomnia 5.13b ★★★** Seven bolts to two-bolt anchor. Ron Kauk with first toprope ascent. Bolted by Dave Wallach, 1997.

East Face of Main Rock, left side

East Face of Main Rock, right side

West Face of Main Rock, Mickey's Beach

10.   **Beach Arête 5.13b ★★★** Seven bolts to two-bolt anchor. Clip the first bolt of *Naked and Disfigured*, then travel up the left edge of the arête. Unfortunately there is a drilled pocket halfway up this stellar line. Tide dependent.

West Face

11.   **Naked and Disfigured 5.12d ★★★★★** Eight bolts to two-bolt anchor. First crux midway up the route, then technical stemming to the top. Kenny Ariza, 1994.

12.   **Mutiny 5.13a ★★** Eight bolts to two-bolt anchor. The low section of the face is classic. A long route on good quality rock. Kenny Ariza, 1997.

13.   **Hot Tuna 5.11d ★★** Five bolts to two rusty old cold shuts. Thin and bouldery. Use first bolt of *Mutiny*, then follow four more bolts up and right.

14.   **Sharky's Machine 5.12a ★★★** Uses *Hot Tuna* anchors (rusty and scary) for toproping. Follow a straight line upward from the base of the rock.

15.   **Motion in the Ocean 5.12d ★★** Seven bolts to two-bolt anchor. Technical, vertical climbing. Kenny Ariza, 1995.

16.   **Gidget Meets the Turgid Sea Monster 5.12d ★★★★** Five bolts to two-bolt anchor shared with *Motion*. An easier variation clips the first 3 bolts on *Gidget*, then goes left and up the last two bolts on *Motion*. This is a five-star 5.12b. Jim Thornburg, 1980s.

17.   **Sturgeon 5.12c ★★★** Six bolts to one-bolt anchor. Take advantage of the rest before tackling the crux bulge two-thirds of the way up.

18.   **Scurvy (a.k.a. Rock Lobster) 5.12c/d ★★★★** Eight bolts to one-bolt anchor. Jim Thornburg toproped this and called it *Scurvy*. Kenny Ariza later bolted it and called it *Rock Lobster*. Both names are currently used. Bolted by Kenny Ariza, 1995.

19.   **Unknown 5.12a ★** Six bolts to two-bolt anchor.

20.   **Nancy 5.11d ★★★★** Six bolts to three-bolt anchor. Pumpy moves up to an overhanging crux past fourth bolt. Beware! The bolts on this route were recently replaced and there are concerns about whether they are solid. Jim Thornburg, 1980s.

21.   **Squid Vicious 5.13a ★★★** Five bolts to three-bolt anchor shared with *Sex Porpoises* and *Nancy*. Last three bolts shared with *Sex Porpoises*.

Southwest Face of Main Rock, Mickey's Beach

Grey Slab, Mickey's Beach

22.   **Sex Porpoises 5.12c ★★★★★** Six bolts to three-bolt anchor. Very popular route. Both strength and fancy footwork needed. Tricky and bouldery. Jim Thornburg, 1980s.

GREY SLAB

Two lines are on the slab. This 25-foot rock (tide dependent) is northwest of the Main Rock. Most people choose to walk off the top of the slab on the northern edge. If rappelling down from the anchor chains, it is a little difficult to get down without your rope getting wet.

1.   **Rust Never Sleeps 5.10a ★★★★** Two bolts to a three-bolt anchor. Cruise up and left past a right-facing crack. The flake below the bolts can be protected with gear if necessary. Clip the first bolt and continue left over small holds that require balance and careful foot placement.

Dave Buchanon on Rust Never Sleeps, *Grey Slab*

Peeper Rock, Mickey's Beach

2. **Unknown 5.9 ★★** Two bolts to a two-bolt anchor. Doesn't compare with *Rust*, but still a fun line.

PEEPER ROCK

This rock got its name due to its great location for checking out all the naked people on Red Rock Beach. It has a two-bolt route up the face with a two-bolt anchor. The highest point of the rock has a very old and very sketchy bolt for toproping the overhang. If you are facing the water, this rock is just right of Main Rock. It is 24 feet high. The route on the east face goes at 5.9. This route can be climbed at high tide since it is on the east face of the rock.

THE EGG

This rock was referred to as Whales Back in the 1970s and possibly into the early 1980s. It holds the newest routes at Mickey's Beach. There are currently eight routes on the rock. The Egg is only a short stroll from Steep Ravine Cabins, located less than 0.5 mile south of Main Rock at Mickey's.

Approach: There are three different ways to approach The Egg. The easiest way is via the paved road that leads from CA 1 down to Steep Ravine Cabins. The gate is locked with a combination that only the employees and people using the cabins and campsites have, but it is perfectly okay to walk around the gate and follow the winding road down to the beach. Facing toward the sea, head down the stairs to the right onto the beach, which is often vacant, except for the occasional crab or starfish. The Egg is located only 100 yards down the beach next to the water.

The Egg, East Face

A shorter (and steeper) way to The Egg follows a narrow foot trail from Shoreline/CA 1 down to the beach. This is the preferred path for people who have healthy knees and are in a hurry to climb. The trailhead is midway between the main parking lot and the paved road leading to Steep Ravine Cabins. Walking along the west side of CA 1, look for a large drainage pipe coming out from underneath the highway. The trail begins below the pipe and winds down to the beach. Turn left when you get to the beach and walk 125 yards to The Egg.

The third approach takes you south 0.5 mile along the beach from Main Rock at Mickey's Beach to The Egg. To travel this somewhat treacherous route, you need to cross numerous slippery, wet boulders, as well as an unstable saddle of sediment that is connected to the sea cliff. This wave-cut portion of terrace is crumbly, loose, and often wet. The other approaches are usually faster.

East Face
1. **Egg Face 5.9** ★★★ Two bolts to one-bolt rappel anchor. Short line but good introductory climb or warm-up.

2. **Unknown 5.6** ★★★★ Two bolts to one-bolt rappel anchor shared with Egg Face. Short but a very nice view to the right.

North Face
3. **Egghead 5.11b** ★★★★★ Six bolts to two-bolt anchor. This route has been called 5.11b for so long, it has been decided by Mickey's diehards that the rating stays although many Bay Area climbers admit to this being the most difficult 5.11b that they have ever climbed. The crux is getting

Nick Fain

The Egg, North Face

off the deck. The handholds aren't too bad, but the feet . . . what feet? If you can get past the second bolt, you are in business; and liebacking the stellar arête makes it all worthwhile.

4. **Junglework 5.12a** ★★ This toprope line uses the *Egghead* anchors. Follow the *Egghead* line just past the second bolt, then veer right 5 feet and go straight up.

5. **This is Your Brain on Drugs 5.12b** ★★★★★ Seven bolts to a two-bolt anchor. A left-hand sloper past the first bolt wakes you up. Crimp off a

Chris Summit on This is Your Brain on Drugs, *The Egg, Mickey's Beach*

The Egg, West Face

small edge with your right paw and lunge right to a decent match, keeping in mind that you have no feet. This crux is before the third bolt. The remainder of the ride is a sustained slabbarific crimpfest. Kenny Ariza, 1999.

6.   **Sign Language 5.10c ★★★★★** Eight bolts to two-bolt anchor. A beautiful line that is tide dependent. Perfect for a sunset. Heads up and follows the right edge of the rock overlooking the sea. Don't go too far right or you will grapple with loose junk. Not exactly the easiest belay stance. Kenny Ariza and Gene Hull, 2000.

West Face

7.   **Sunnyside Up 5.11a ★★** Seven bolts to two-bolt anchor. The rock on this line is crumbly in a few sections with a sandier geologic composition. Crux off the deck, then easier climbing awaits. Tide dependent. Kenny Ariza and Eppie Ordaz, 2000.

8.   **Shell Shock 5.12c ★★★** Six bolts to two-bolt anchor shared with *Sunnyside Up*. Stick-clip the first bolt. Climb a V6 crux at base, then finishes up with 5.10 climbing. Also tide dependent. Kenny Ariza, 2000.

CALIFORNIA SLAB

This large slab is rarely climbed and has large quantities of lichen on it. Caution should be taken since certain sections are crumbly. The main crack on the west face is almost 80 feet long and goes at 5.9. To the right of the large main crack, there is a shorter off-width crack, also rated 5.9.

California Slab, Mickey's Beach

The majority of the climbing is done on the slab section on the left side of the main crack. Various lines here range from 5.7 to 5.10a. The slab is next to Steep Ravine Cabins on the hillside facing the ocean. You will see it when walking past the cabins to The Egg.

ENDLESS BUMMER ROCK

This extremely overhanging rock has two routes on it. Neither route is tide-dependent. The rock has a much higher concentration of sandstone than Main Rock and The Egg. The trailhead is located 1.1 miles south of the main parking lot. Park in the small dirt pullout, which can hold four or five cars. Be sure to use your odometer since there are several small pullouts close to one another.

Approach: Head west on the trail leading directly from the pullout to the ridge. Continue along the ridge as far as it goes. You will be overlooking the water. Walk to your left and down on a prominent trail, which will lead directly to the top of Endless Bummer Rock. Walk around and down the north edge of it to the routes.

1.   **Endless Bummer 5.13b ★★★★** Seven bolts to two rusty cold shuts. Small Swiss cheese-like pockets lead you off the ground. The line heads up and right. Intense overhang.

2.   **Surf Safari 5.14a ★★★** Seven bolts to a two-bolt anchor.

BOULDERING

Excellent bouldering awaits you at Mickey's Beach and Stinson Beach. Many difficult overhanging problems exist in the V6-V11 range, but easier problems are available on many boulders as well. Marin County resident and climber

Endless Bummer Rock, West Face

Northfacing view of the overhanging Endless Bummer Rock

Stinson Beach Boulders with Are You Experienced Boulder on the far right

Russell Bobzien discovered bouldering potential here as early as 1977.

Various boulders are located north of Main Rock and scattered along Red Rock Beach and Stinson Beach for 0.5 mile. It is easier to access the boulders on Stinson Beach, walking south from Stinson rather than walking north from Mickey's, because a barrier of rocks that is often immersed in water splits Mickey's (Red Rock) and Stinson Beach. The ever-popular boulder "Are You Experienced" rests at the far south end of Stinson Beach, close to the hillside. The complete traverse on this rock from left to right goes at V11. Danger Boulder, also known as Orange Budda Boulder, is another popular boulder at Mickey's Beach.

Russell Bobzien on Are You Experienced Boulder

Danger Boulder, also known as Orange Budda Boulder

Climbing legend Allen Steck still going strong on I–12, Indian Rock, Berkeley

East Bay and San Francisco Areas

BERKELEY AREAS

If you are an East Bay resident and have been climbing for even a short period of time, chances are good you have bouldered or climbed at one of the very popular crags in the Berkeley hills. You won't find any exceptionally breathtaking views or airy exposed climbs here, but you will find a wide variety of bouldering and toprope climbing that appeals to everyone from ultra-beginner to expert. The climbing areas covered in this section are all within 2 miles of each other.

The appeal of the rock around Berkeley has helped enrich its history. Many of climbing's "Old Timers" have used this as a training camp before conquering the walls of Yosemite and beyond. Jules Eichorn, the first ascentionist of the Higher Cathedral Spire, Allen Steck (Steck-Salathe), Steve Roper (wrote and published the first Yosemite climbing guide in 1964), Chuck Pratt, and Royal Robbins all practiced their skills and strained their lats on these rock formations.

Area Geology: The rocks scattered across the Berkeley hills are rhyolites. Rhyolites are volcanic rocks with a high concentration of silica. The silica content associates them with continental volcanos rather than oceanic volcanos. The rocks are extrusive, meaning that the lava cooled quickly due to its exposure to air. When rhyolite is light gray or whitish in color, such as most of the rock in Berkeley, it is felsic rhyolite, which contains a greater percentage of quartz, micas, and silicate mixtures than darker mafic rocks such as basalt and gabbro. Mafic rocks are igneous rocks rich in magnesium and iron. The rock in and around Berkeley is estimated to be about 100 million years old.

TRIP INFORMATION

Note: Information on water and restrooms is listed under each climbing area.

Climbing Season: Cool temperatures are common here, even in July and August, with an average summertime high of only 70 degrees. Climbing in Berkeley is basically a year-round activity. Hats and fleece will help between November and April. The average high temperature in Berkeley in the winter months is 56 degrees.

Fees: There are no fees at any of the crags in this section.

Camping: Tilden Regional Park has four separate campgrounds located in the Berkeley hills. Call (510) 562–PARK for more information.

Dogs: Dogs must be on leash in parks and climbing areas. Citations may be issued.

Emergency Services: The nearest hospital for emergency care is Alta-Bates Medical Center, located on Ashby Avenue at the corner of Telegraph Avenue. There is service available twenty-four hours. Call (510) 204–1303, or (510) 204–4444.

Telephones: There are no public telephones at any of the climbing areas. In dire emergencies, you could try nearby residences; and at Grizzly Peak, the Lawrence Hall of Science may be the swiftest method of getting to a phone to dial for help.

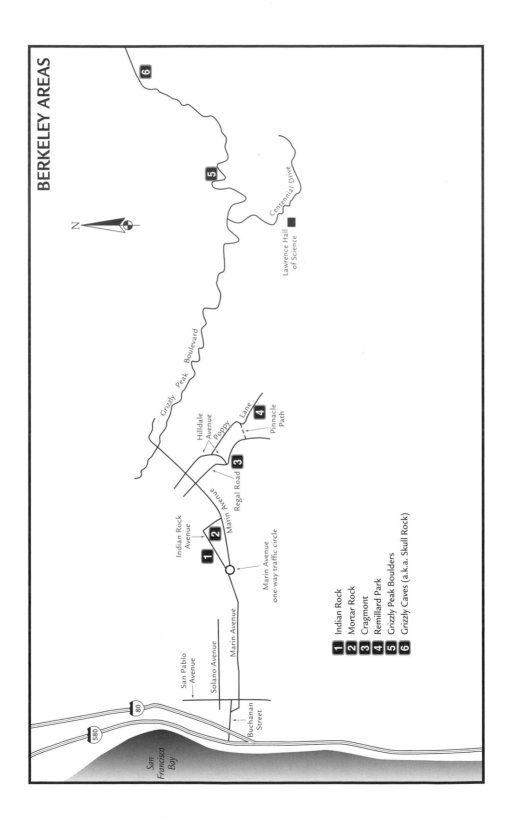

BERKELEY AREAS

N

1 Indian Rock
2 Mortar Rock
3 Cragmont
4 Remillard Park
5 Grizzly Peak Boulders
6 Grizzly Caves (a.k.a. Skull Rock)

San Francisco Bay

580

80

San Pablo Avenue

Solano Avenue

Marin Avenue

Buchanan Street

Indian Rock Avenue

Marin Avenue

Marin Avenue one-way traffic circle

1
2

Grizzly Peak Boulevard

Hilldale Avenue

Poppy Lane

Regal Road

Pinnacle Path

3
4

5

6

Centennial Drive

Lawrence Hall of Science

Coffee Shops: Berkeley is known for its youthful college atmosphere, coffee houses, and poetry readings. Several sources for coffee are located within a mile or 2 of the climbing areas. Peet's is located on Solano Avenue near the intersection of Colusa Avenue. Head down Shattuck Avenue at the traffic circle.

Markets: There is an Andronico's on Solano Avenue between Fresno Avenue and Colusa Avenue. A full deli is located inside.

Brewpubs: Jupiter Brewery on Shattuck Avenue in Berkeley is a popular spot for a good reason. The restaurant has twenty-five beers on tap, reasonably priced but more than simply pub food, an outdoor patio, and often times, live jazz. From Indian Rock Avenue near the traffic circle, drive around the fountain and turn right (south) onto Sutter Street. Sutter becomes Henry Street and within two more blocks becomes Shattuck Avenue. Jupiter Brewery is at 2181 Shattuck Avenue (at Center Street).

Pyramid Brewery is located in Berkeley not far from the climbing areas. Lunch and dinner is available, and the beer is above average. It is located at the corner of Gilman Street and Eighth Street, 7 blocks east of I–80.

Gas Stations: The closest station to the climbing areas is a Chevron, located next to the Andronico's on Solano Avenue at Colusa Avenue.

Directions: From San Francisco, take Interstate 80 (eastbound) over the Bay Bridge. Continue east through Berkeley, exit at Buchanan Street/Albany, and turn left on Buchanan. Go 3 blocks and veer right onto Marin Avenue. Follow this road east, passing the Alameda, until you reach an obvious one way traffic

circle with a fountain in the center of it. Follow the circle to the opposite side. Here you will need to turn right on Indian Rock Avenue or turn right on Marin Avenue depending on which area you are visiting. See further directions under each climbing area.

INDIAN ROCK

Definitely the most popular area in Berkeley, Indian Rock offers countless boulder problems and a handful of short, toprope routes. Freestanding boulders next to the road offer hard overhanging problems, and toproping is available on the upper northernmost section of rock.

To set up topropes, walk up the stairs carved into the rock and head right. An old bolt is used for an

Chi-Chih Lin traversing the rihyolite at Indian Rock   anchor, but it should be backed up

INDIAN ROCK

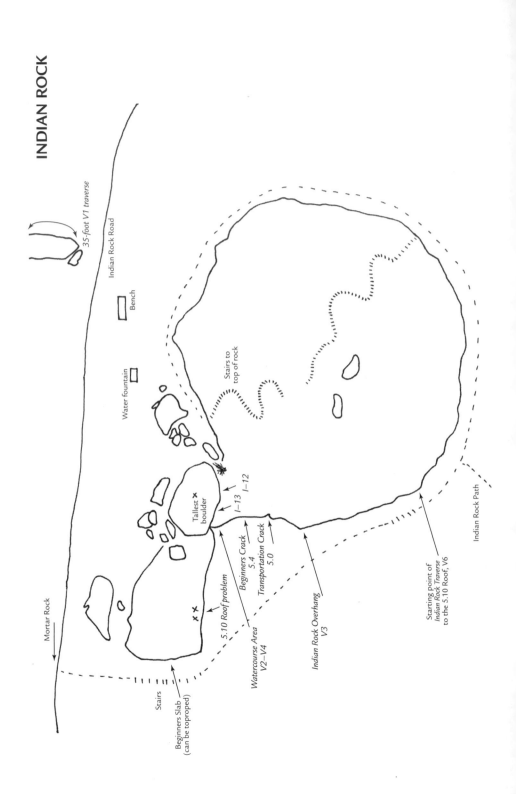

35-foot V1 traverse

Indian Rock Road

Bench

Water fountain

Stairs to
top of rock

Mortar Rock

Tallest ✕
boulder

I–13

I–12

5.10 Roof problem

Beginners Crack
5.4

Transportation Crack
5.0

Watercourse Area
V2–V4

Indian Rock Overhang
V3

Stairs

Beginners Slab
(can be toproped)

Indian Rock Path

Starting point of
Indian Rock Traverse
to the 5.10 Roof, V6

with traditional gear. There are two lines on the highest section of rock. Facing the rock, I-12 is on the right and I-13 is on the left. You will find more bolts above a nice overhanging roof problem, which is located on the left edge of the pit. The problem tops out at 15 feet. Across the street from Indian Rock is a 35-foot traverse on a boulder that stands just over 10 feet high. The traverse goes at V1. A few additional problems are shown on Indian Rock on the map on page 92.

Water Sources: A water fountain is available in front of Indian Rock.

Restrooms: Although desperately needed at the heavily visited Indian Rock, no bathrooms are available. You can either head up the hill to Cragmont, or take the low road back down to the busy shopping area on Solano Avenue. From Marin Avenue at Indian Rock Avenue, head west on Marin Avenue and turn right on the Alameda, then turn left on Solano Avenue.

Directions: From the traffic circle, head right (uphill) on Indian Rock Avenue for less than 0.5 mile. Indian Rock Park will be on your left-hand side. A convenient footpath is behind Indian Rock Park. (The path is fittingly called Indian Rock Path.) The path winds directly down to Solano Avenue at the corner of The Alameda, where you'll find shops and restaurants nearby.

Approach: Park on Indian Rock Avenue or San Mateo Road. The largest amount of bouldering is available at the bottom of the stairs.

MORTAR ROCK

Mortar Rock is best known for the overhanging *Nat's Traverse*, which goes at V8. There are many difficult problems on the main chunk of tuff, including *Jungle Fever* and *Nat's Lyback*. There are easier bouldering problems on the smaller boulders across the path from Mortar Rock. Little Half Dome is the tallest of the three boulders and has problems ranging from V0 to V3. The southernmost boulder, though small, has *Pipeline Traverse* that goes at V4.

Water Sources: There are no water sources at Mortar Rock. Walk 50 yards to Indian Rock Park where a water fountain exists.

Restrooms: There are no restrooms close to Mortar Rock. Check the directions for Cragmont, where a public restroom is available.

Directions: From the traffic circle, head right (uphill) on Indian Rock Avenue for 0.5 mile. Mortar Rock is on your right, just past Indian Rock Park.

Bill Granados on Nat's Traverse, Mortar Rock

MORTAR ROCK

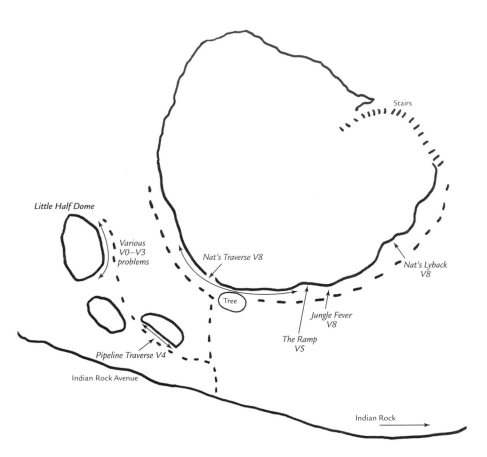

Stairs

Little Half Dome

Various
V0–V3
problems

Nat's Traverse V8

Nat's Lyback
V8

Tree

Jungle Fever
V8

The Ramp
V5

Pipeline Traverse V4

Indian Rock Avenue

Indian Rock

CRAGMONT

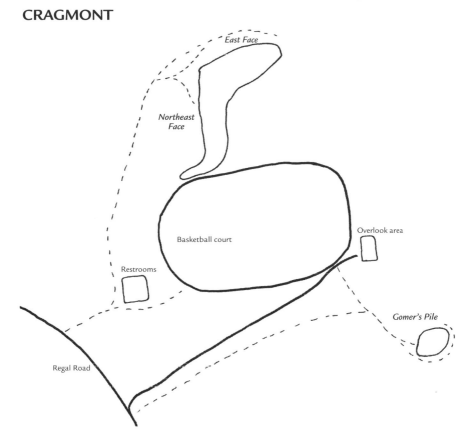

CRAGMONT

Cragmont is a popular first-time outdoor climbing crag for many folks in the East Bay. Several toprope routes exist, as well as a short, bolted 5.11c. Behind the basketball courts and overlook area is a shaded boulder (often referred to as Gomer's Pile) with a V7 traverse.

Water Sources: A water fountain is available at Cragmont.

Restrooms: A public restroom is available at Cragmont. Rubber gloves and a gas mask are recommended.

Directions: From the traffic circle, continue up Marin Avenue and turn right on Regal Road. The park will be on your right-hand side. Crag-hopping? There is a quaint little walkway between Cragmont and Remillard Park called Pinnacle Path (see overview map).

Northeast Face

All routes on this face are toprope problems except *Beginners Crack*.

1.   Face 5.8 ★★ Toprope face straight up over a small bulge.

CRAGMONT, NORTHEAST FACE

2. **Beginners Crack 5.6** ★★★ Good route for beginners.

3. **Face to Crack 5.7** ★ Toprope route. Start in center of rock at the base and climb up and left to crack and anchors.

4. **Undercling Crack 5.7** ★★★ Climb up and right, following the huge undercling to the anchors. Likely the most popular route at Cragmont.

5. **Moss Ledge 5.10b** ★★★★ Small holds incorporated with a bulge make this a challenging route. Leigh Ortenburger (in mountaineering boots), 1955.

6. **Face 5.9** ★★ Start below and right of the anchors and go up and left.

East Face

7. **Face 5.10d R** ★★ Go up and left past a bolt to a three-bolt anchor.

8. **Bolt Route 5.11c** ★★ Four bolts to three-bolt anchor. Easy climbing to first bolt, then climb up and over an overhanging bulge just below the lip.

CRAGMONT, EAST FACE

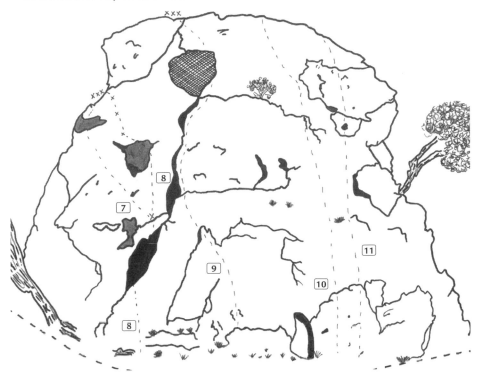

9. **Farewell to Arms 5.10a ★★★★** Climb up and right, following a crack system to a large hueco. The crux is near the overhanging section near the top.

10. **Face 5.10b ★★** This route has much smaller holds than Farewell but less of an overhang.

11. **Cave Route 5.8 ★★** Climb up and left of the tree past the cave-like feature to the top.

REMILLARD PARK

This rock formation in the Berkeley hills is a great picnic spot and seldom will you see more than a handful of people here. Often shady, the north-facing crag is a great place for a hot summer day because it very rarely gets too warm for climbing. There is also potential for new routes if the rock is cleared and cleaned of lichen in spots.

The main chunk of welded tuff facing Poppy Lane is about 25 feet and has a pipe secured on top for toproping. Bring extra long slings and thick skin (the tuff is hard on the fingers). A couple bolts have been cut from the face, so currently most routes must be toproped. The highest formation is in the rear and has two bolts on the top for an anchor. One of these bolts has already seen its heyday and as of this writing should be avoided. Fortunately, cracks are available nearby for gear placement to supplement the solid bolt.

The smallest chunk of tuff is located closest to the street and has a park plaque on the face of it. This rock actually features quality routes on it, though they are only 14 feet high. Three solid bolts are atop this rock for toproping and are easily reached by climbing up the backside of the rock.

Water Sources: BYOW. There is none available at the park.

Allison Reilly going vertical on Remillard Park

Restrooms: Too bad you cannot bring your own restroom to the park. The closest facility is at Cragmont.

Directions: From the traffic circle, continue up Marin Avenue and turn right on Hilldale Avenue. Turn left on Poppy Lane where you'll find Remillard Park on the right near the end of the street.

PINNACLE ROCK

These routes top out at 25 feet, and most lines must be toproped.

1. **Crack 5.8 ★★★** This route requires a brief lieback. It tops out at about 20 feet at a small tree.

2. **Face 5.11+ ★★** This route begins 2 feet right of the crack. Thin, balancey, and challenging. A couple of cut bolts are on this line.

3. **Face 5.10d ★★★★** Start 4 feet right of the crack and use small pockets on this overhanging route.

4. **Bucket Prow 5.6 ★★★★** A fun warm-up on hueco-like buckets.

5. **Overhanging Buckets 5.10a ★★★★** Another fun overhanging route.

6. **Overhang 5.10c ★★** This route is a bit reachy and a little dirty in various pockets.

belay pole

6

5

4

3

2

1

Pinnacle Rock, Remillard Park

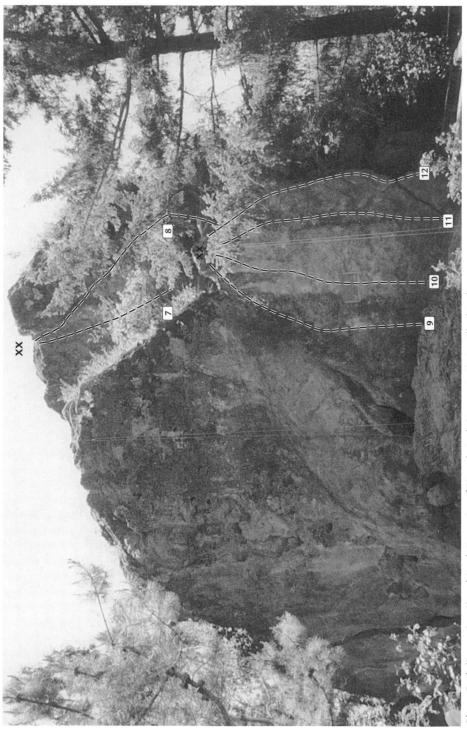

Plaque Rock (Routes 9–12) and South Formation of Pinnacle Rock (Routes 7–8), Remillard Park

SOUTH FORMATION

Although the tallest section of rock, this formation has the least amount of routes on it.

7. Slabby 5.9 ★Smooth surface area makes this otherwise easy-shmeezy toprope route a little tricky.

8. Crack 5.7 ★★★ This short left-leaning crack is good practice for the real stuff.

PLAQUE ROCK

These are all toprope problems.

9. Arête 5.7 ★★ Fun route using the face of the rock for the right foot and hand.

10. Face 5.11c ★★★ Up and over the plaque itself, this route goes straight to the top on greasy crimpers.

11. Face 5.11b ★★ Go right of the plaque and straight up. Balance and strong fingers are a must.

12. Face 5.10a ★★★★ Great route. Takes a good eye to see the better hand-holds that lead up the right side to the anchors.

GRIZZLY PEAK BOULDERS

If you live or work in the vicinity of Grizzly Peak, this area is worth visiting. Otherwise, it may not be worth the trip. For starters, poison oak is lurking beside every boulder and ready to attack. Be aware that in the past the area has been used as an illegal campsite and toilet.

GRIZZLY PEAK BOULDERS

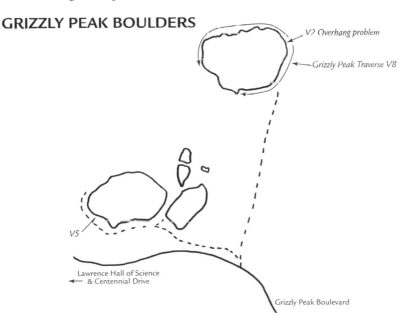

V2 Overhang problem

Grizzly Peak Traverse V8

V5

Lawrence Hall of Science & Centennial Drive

Grizzly Peak Boulevard

Water Sources: There is no water source near the boulders. The Lawrence Hall of Science at Centennial Drive and Grizzly Peak Boulevard is your closest option.

Restrooms: No public restrooms are available at the boulders.

Directions: From the traffic circle, continue up Marin Avenue and turn right on Grizzly Peak Boulevard. Drive past Centennial Drive, where the Lawrence Hall of Science is located. From the intersection of Grizzly Peak and Centennial, go 0.3 mile to the first outcropping of rock on the left-hand side. This is easy to miss when traveling in this direction (east) but quite visible off the side of the road when traveling west.

GRIZZLY CAVES (A.K.A. SKULL ROCK)

Two rocks exist here. The main rock has a prominent cave on one side where you will find most of the climbing. The highest point of the rock is 35 feet. There is a smaller rock next to the main rock, but it reaches less than 20 feet.

Skull Rock might have been a good climbing destination a decade or two ago, but now it is trashed. Beer cans, broken bottles, and other garbage is often strewn everywhere. Worse yet, fires burned at the base of rock inside the cave have covered the main rock with a thick coat of nasty soot. As you may have guessed, the site is a popular spot for partiers, taggers, and others who do not respect outdoor ethics. This makes a rather depressing climbing experience for most.

Climbing ranges from 5.8 to 5.10. Bolts are set atop the main rock for toproping. Optimistic climbers can ascend on the backside opposite the cave.

Water Sources: Be sure to take water with you to Grizzly Caves. No spigot or fountain is available.

GRIZZLY CAVES

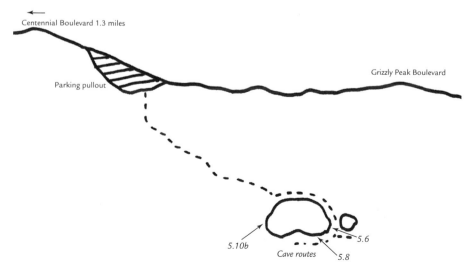

Restrooms: The Lawrence Hall of Science on Centennial Drive and Grizzly Peak Boulevard is the closest restroom to the Grizzly Caves.

Directions: From the traffic circle, continue up Marin Avenue and turn right on Grizzly Peak Boulevard. Continue past Centennial Drive, where the Lawrence Hall of Science is located. From the intersection of Grizzly Peak and Centennial, go 1.3 miles to Grizzly Caves. Park in the pullout on your right. Follow the trail downhill and left to this 50-foot chunk of rhyolite, often referred to as Skull Rock.

Leeta Steenwyk on Jungle Book, *Boy Scout Rocks, Mount Diablo*

MOUNT DIABLO STATE PARK

Mount Diablo State Park is known for cycling, hiking, climbing, and above all its vast views from the 3,849-foot summit. Overlooking primarily California's Central Valley, the panoramic view is thought to be unsurpassed by any other in America, and second only to Mount Kilimanjaro as the world's most panoramic. To the north, Mount Lassen is visible in the Cascades. To the south, Mount Loma Prieta ascends in the Santa Cruz Mountains. To the southeast, Mount Hamilton is visible; and on a very clear day (unfortunately such days seem rarer these days), you might see Half Dome in the Yosemite Valley if a pair of binoculars is handy. Furthermore, an astute sightseer might make out landmarks in at least thirty-five of California's fifty-eight counties.

Mount Diablo offers good climbing in a setting not far from the hustle and bustle of the city. Located just 2 miles east of Walnut Creek, the park is nice for a day trip or a weekend get-away. Climbing is located near the south end of Mount Diablo State Park at Boy Scout Rocks, which reach up to 91 feet. There are also some taller, less crowded formations (which tend to be lower quality) known as Pine Canyon. This crag, located on the border of Mount Diablo State Park and Castle Rock Regional Park, has routes reaching up to 150 feet.

Most of the climbing at Boy Scout Rocks is toproping, but five bolted, sporty routes exist on the north face of the Lower Tier. Climbers can traditionally lead the cracks, but due to the nature of the sandstone, most choose to toprope these climbs. Unfortunately, many bolts on Butt Rock, Upper Tier, and Middle Tier have been cut. A solid toprope anchor for some of the routes at Upper Tier now requires webbing (or better yet, another rope) reaching 30 feet, in order to cover the distance from a lone tree back out over the edge of the face.

Area Geology: Geologists claim Diablo is a "pop-up" structure, meaning there is most likely a thrust fault underneath the area caused by compression at right angles to the coastal ranges. The compression pushed the formations upward. Basically all of the coastal ranges are uplifted by thrust faults and the folding of rocks, but there is a gap in the coastal ranges around the San Francisco Bay Area. Mount Diablo is the only site pushed up in this gap.

There are interesting formations in the park, with everything from greenstone and reddish chert cliffs to greywacke sandstone and shale caves. Sandstone is the main formation in the park and the type of rock that is developed and climbed. The sandstone rests in bands across the terrain. The reason bands of stone are formed is due to the sandstone being laid down in layers, which are later tilted up and eroded. Since some layers erode easier and faster than others, the edges of the sandstone beds become the rock bands we climb on. The rock is so soft in certain areas that deep grooves have been made from rope rubbing over edges. Some grooves are 3 inches deep on the Middle Tier at Boy Scout Rocks. The oldest rock in the park is around 190 million years old.

After a heavy rain, the sandstone needs sufficient time to completely dry out. Please allow at least two full days of dry skies before climbing so as to not risk losing any key holds at the crag. Also note that traditional pro may not fix as solid in sandstone as it does in other rock types.

TRIP INFORMATION

Climbing Season: Mount Diablo is a great cold weather crag because it lies east of the coast. Warmer temperatures in the late spring and summer mean much of the better climbing is done in the morning or late afternoon. It is possible to move with the shade at Boy Scout Rocks, climbing in certain sections of Upper Tier and Middle Tier when Lower Tier is saturated in sun. Temperatures here are often 10 to 20 degrees warmer than in the city.

In the cooler months, Boy Scout gives a little more shelter from wind than Pine Canyon. The average high temperature here in the dead of winter is 55 degrees. Note: The park is subject to closure during the summer months due to fire danger. Call ahead at (925) 837–2525.

Fees: Day-use fee at Mount Diablo State Park is $2.00 per vehicle, and Castle Rock Regional Park is free.

Camping: Diablo has three camping areas with a total of sixty-four sites. Two of these campgrounds, Juniper and Live Oak, require reservations, while the third, Junction Campground, offers sites on a first-come, first-served basis. Off-season camping (between October 1 and May 31) is $12 per night, and sites during the busy season (June 1 to September 30) are $16 per night. Extra vehicles are charged $5.00. Free showers are provided at Live Oak and Juniper. Reservations can be made by calling (800) 444–7275. On-line reservations can be made at www.parks.ca.gov.

Dogs: Dogs are only allowed on-leash at the camgrounds at Mount Diablo State Park. They are not permitted on any trails. If climbing at Pine Canyon, inside the boundaries of Castle Rock Regional Park, bring Fido along. Dogs are allowed if they are leashed.

Emergency Services: The closest medical facility to the park is John Muir Medical Center in Walnut Creek. The quickest way to the hospital is to exit the park through the north gate. If leaving Castle Rock, head back toward Walnut Avenue. The hospital is located on Ygnacio Valley Road at La Casa Via Drive, less than 0.5 mile west of Walnut Avenue. The phone number is (925) 939–3000.

If departing the south end of the park, go to San Ramon Regional Medical Center, located in San Ramon on the corner of Alcosta Boulevard and Norris Canyon Road, 0.5 mile east of Interstate 680. The phone is (925) 275–9200.

Water Sources: There are plenty of spigots and fountains in the park. The majority of them are directly off the side of South Gate and North Gate Roads.

Telephones: Phones are located in the boundaries of the park at the Junction Ranger Station and at the summit of Mount Diablo.

Restrooms: Five restroom facilities are available in the park. The closest one to Boy Scout Rocks is at the parking lot for Rock City. The closest restroom to Pine Canyon is east of the parking lot near the entrance to Castle Rock Regional Park.

Coffee Shops: If you are using the north entrance into Mount Diablo State Park, you are in luck. Peet's is located on Ygnacio Valley Road at La Casa Via in the Oak Grove Plaza. The nearest cross street is Walnut Avenue. Conveniently enough, Sonoma Valley Bagel Co. is directly next door to Peet's.

For climbers entering or exiting the south end of the park, Danville Coffee Roastery is close by. Take Diablo Road west off I–680, go 3 blocks, and turn right on Hartz Avenue. The roastery is on your right-hand side. The address is 290 Hartz Avenue.

Markets: If entering the south end of the park, there is an Albertsons located on the north side of Diablo Road, a half block west of I–680.

Bound for Pine Canyon? In the same shopping center in Walnut Creek as Peet's and the Sonoma Valley Bagel Co., there is an Albertsons, and also a Rite-Aid Pharmacy.

Brewpubs: Black Diamond Brewing Company is at the corner of North Main Street and Parkside Drive in Walnut Creek. The beer is great and so too is the grub. The atmosphere is casual, and on Friday and Saturday nights there is live music.

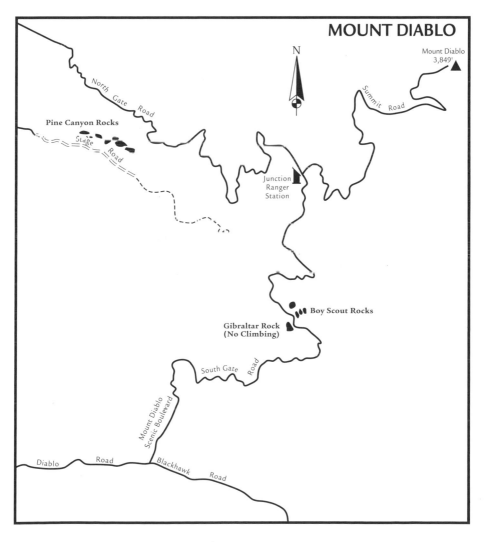

To get there from the north gate of Diablo or from Pine Canyon, head back toward the freeway on Ygnacio Valley Road. Two blocks before I-680, you will need to turn right onto North Main Street. Go 2 long blocks to where Parkside Drive intersects. Black Diamond is on your right-hand side. The brewpub is named after a mining company that did business in Walnut Creek in past years.

Gas Stations: If driving through the north end of the park, there are gas stations on Ygnacio Valley Road. If traveling in or out of the south end of the park, Tom's Unocal is located at 400 Diablo Road in Danville at the intersection of I-680.

Directions: If you are climbing at Boy Scout Rocks, it is best to enter the park via South Gate Road. From I-680, exit the freeway in Danville at Diablo Road. Turn left, staying on Diablo Road while it turns to the left and then veers to the right. Follow the signs leading to the park, turning left onto Mount Diablo Scenic Boulevard, which becomes South Gate Road and leads you through the park.

If you are planning on conquering the rock at Pine Canyon in Castle Rock Regional Park, your best bet is passing through Walnut Creek. From I-680 in Walnut Creek, exit at Ygnacio Valley Road. Head east, drive 2.5 miles until you reach Walnut Avenue, where you will turn right. Go 1.5 miles farther and turn right on Oak Grove Road. Oak Grove turns into Castle Rock Road, which will lead you directly into Castle Rock Regional Park.

BOY SCOUT ROCKS

Most folks frequent Boy Scout Rocks rather than Pine Canyon. This crag has been a popular climbing destination for more than thirty years. Many climbers living in the Bay Area have honed their skills and beefed up their biceps and forearms here before heading for the walls of Yosemite.

There are three tiers of rock situated on a gradually sloping hillside. In addition, there is a separate rock 75 yards northwest of these formations called Butt Rock. It tops out at 70 feet.

The tallest formation at Boy Scout Rocks is the lower tier, which reaches 91 feet. This is where you will find the only true bolted sport routes. Unfortunately many bolts have been chopped on the Upper Tier and at Butt Rock (by an unknown scoundrel) leaving some earlier sport climbs now just toproping routes. This has also facilitated the need for extremely long slings for tree anchors (a separate rope is often used) on routes that previously had nice bolts set for toproping. In addition to this annoyance, the bolts on the only protected line up Butt Rock (South Face) were cut as well, which leaves soloing the 5.3 chimney the safest way to the top. Once atop Butt Rock, you can sling a boulder for toproping on all routes and put some chocks in cracks used for backup protection. Long slings are also needed here.

Approach: One reason for the popularity of Boy Scout Rocks is the easy approach. The rocks are located only moments from the road at the south end of the park. After passing through the south gate, continue for 1 mile. There are a small number of parking spaces along the side of the road near Gibraltar Rock.

If these are taken, the parking lot at Rock City is on the northeast (right) side of the road less than 0.5 mile past Gibraltar Rock. There are wooden stairs that lead directly from the road down to Butt Rock. Fifty yards southeast of these stairs, locate a trail next to a cave-like formation covered in huecos that rises to 30 feet. This same trail winds down to all three tiers at the Boy Scout. Following this trail on the north side of Roadside Cave will bring you down to the first tier of rocks, otherwise known as the Upper Tier. To reach the Middle Tier and Lower Tier, continue down the trail heading northeast. Watch out for poison oak.

Upper Tier

For toprope access to these climbs, head up the east side of the rock to the left of *Pebbly Face.*

1. **Pebbly Face 5.10c ★★★★** Toprope route. Start 8 feet left of *Chouinard's Crack* and follow tiny holds up and over a bulge. Try not to use the old bolt hole at the base to pull on, thus making it more challenging.

2. **Chouinard's Crack 5.8 ★★★** Pro to 3″. This crack is deceptive, with the crux less than 20 feet off the deck, aiming to spit you out.

BOY SCOUT ROCKS, UPPER TIER

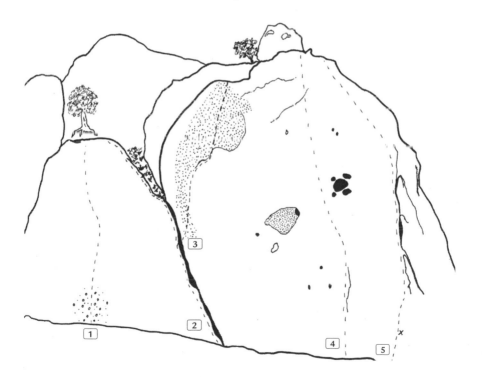

3. **Face 5.10a ★★** <u>Toprope</u> route. Start up *Chouinard's*. Once you pull the crux, climb right onto the face for 5 feet, then continue straight up over a crimpy section and through a short slab to the top.

4. **Old Aid Route A3** Hook? Bat Hook? Beware! Aid climbs change with the time and wearing of the rock surface. Sandstone wears quickly and easily. Two bolts on this line have been cut.

5. **Pie Crust 5.11c ★★** <u>Toprope route</u>. Apparently there used to be six bolts on this route. Now all that remains is one rusty old bolt near the base and some chain anchors close to the top. Getting off the ground is aided (with the old bolt), then it gets easier. The flake is 5.8, then hard face moves lead you to the top.

West Face of Middle Tier

To access the toprope bolts for *Jungle Book* and *In the Buckets*, walk up the sandstone gully on the north side of Middle Tier.

6. **Jungle Book 5.10d ★★★★** Heads up a right-facing crack that requires either good technique or grunting in order to avoid a barn door.

7. **In the Buckets 5.11c/d ★★★★★** <u>Toprope route</u>. Awkward moves on sandy slopers and pinner pinches. Time changes things quickly on sandstone. This used to be a 5.11a until an important flake broke off.

8. **Face 5.7–5.10** Various lines exist over dozens of good pockets.

9. **Crack 5.6 ★★** Start left of the cave and follow a short line to the top.

Barbara Smejkal

Author on In the Buckets, *Middle Tier, Boy Scout Rocks*

WEST FACE OF MIDDLE TIER

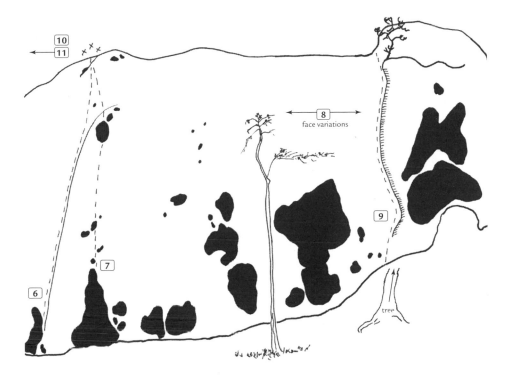

North Face of Middle Tier

Apparently a small tree once stood near the top of the Northern Face of Middle Tier and was commonly used as a toprope anchor. One day an unknowing chap took a hard fall halfway up the rock and the weary tree with its shallow roots was yanked from the sandy soil. The tree tumbled down on top of the lucky man, who escaped with only a broken ankle and maybe a couple of sticks in his ear. These are toprope routes.

10.   Betty's Beard Left 5.11b Might be a good route if moss was cleared from the rock.

11.   Betty's Beard Right 5.11a Ditto of above. Just too much muck.

North Face of Lower Tier

12.   Face 5.10a ★ Use anchor bolts west of Amazing Face anchors for toproping this route.

13.   Crack 5.7 ★★

LOWER TIER

East Face of Lower Tier

To access the top of *Ozone*, climb up the third class south edge of the Lower Tier. Accessing the top of *Amazing Face* requires either going up the gully around the north side of the Lower Tier, or scrambling up the south side.

14. **Ozone 5.10c ★★★★★** Face moves to a chunky flake up and right. Then tackle a roof leading to a short hands and finger crack to the top.

15. **Ozone Direct 5.10d ★★★★★** Toprope route. Start 6 feet right of *Ozone*. Mantle up to a nice ledge, then crimp and edge up and left to the wide crack below the roof of *Ozone*.

16. **Godzilla 5.12 X** Six bolts. No anchors. This line can be toproped from the tree, but you are in store for a huge swing if you come off before traversing right to *Diagonal Crack*. Matt Garner, 1990.

17. **Stegosaurus 5.10b ★★★** Toprope route. Use the right-facing flake to ascend up to *Diagonal Crack*. Follow it a bit and then go straight up to the top.

18. **Diagonal Crack 5.10b ★★★★** Follow the left-facing crack while relying on your left foot for face moves to prevent a barn door. There is a bolt near the top of the crack for added protection if leading.

19. **Face 5.11d R ★★★** Six bolts lead you to nothing but a tree. Easy walk-off. May be a good idea to stick-clip the first bolt because you will be standing on dime-sized edges when clipping in 15 feet off the deck. Meander up the face using tiny edges amid a spattering of slippery moss. The crux is between the second and third bolts, but the climb remains sustained.

20. **Dinosaur 5.11b ★★★** This route lost a couple of bolts somewhere in the past thirty years, so toproping it is the only option. Follows the face just left of the chimney. Diagonal moves to the left cause frequent barn-dooring. The crux is 10 feet above the dirt.

21. **Chimney 5.7 ★★** Definitely more fun than the chimney on the east face of Butt Rock.

22. **Amazing Face 5.9 ★★★★** Eleven bolts to three-bolt anchor on top. Great feet and an abundance of holds, coupled with 91 feet of sandstone, make this the most popular route at Boy Scout Rocks. Walk off.

23. **Bolt Route 5.10b ★★★★★** Eight bolts leading to chains. The crux on this climb is just getting off the ground. A committing move lies just past the last bolt. If you still have juice at the chains, continue up and right past the upper three bolts of *Earthcling* to the top. 75 feet.

24. **Earthcling (a.k.a. Dire Blow) 5.11b ★★★★** Five bolts lead to chains. Very difficult crux before first bolt. Climbing gets much easier above the second bolt. This route originally only had four bolts; but when new bolts were placed by an unknown party, another bolt was added for protection. It is possible the climbers who replaced the bolts called the route *Dire Blow* because they did not know the first ascentionist had previously named it *Earthcling*. Edwin Drummond (bolted on lead with a hand drill), 1984.

BUTT ROCK

West Face
Routes on Butt Rock are usually anchored by either using gear in cracks on top, slinging the boulder on top, or if climbing on the west face, using the tree as an anchor.

25. **Cave Route 5.10b ★★** Toprope route. Short stint over slopey bulges to the top. 20 feet.

South Face
The face climbs are toprope problems.

26. **Left Face 5.7 ★**

South Face of Butt Rock

27.   Center Face 5.8 ★★

28.   Right Face 5.8 ★★

29.   Chimney 5.3 The safest way (not the easiest, nor the most exciting) to the top in order to set anchors.

North Face

30.   Chimney 5.7 ★ Ouch.

31.   Crack-A-No-Go Does Go 5.11c ★★ This overhanging finger crack heads up and right while gradually widening to hands. Good luck trusting your pro here. A good line to put a friend on who flashes all your projects.

PINE CANYON

Pine Canyon is not a hugely popular climbing destination for two main reasons. First, the approach is fairly long and arduous. Second, there are many sections of rock that are crumbly, flakey sandstone. It is common for holds to break off this often papier-mâché-like surface. The sandstone here must be scrutinized before placing gear and take care using any of the ancient bolts that are commonly found in the park.

With that said, there are a handful of decent routes on solid sections of rock. The issue in question is whether the hike in and the hunt for various routes will be worth your time and energy. In past years, Pine Canyon was intermittingly closed for climbing between February and June due to the possible impact on rare birds nesting in the area. There are currently no restrictions and no plans for restrictions in the future. Heads up for swallows defending their nesting grounds. Some climbs travel within inches of their homes, and these birds are feisty.

PINE CANYON

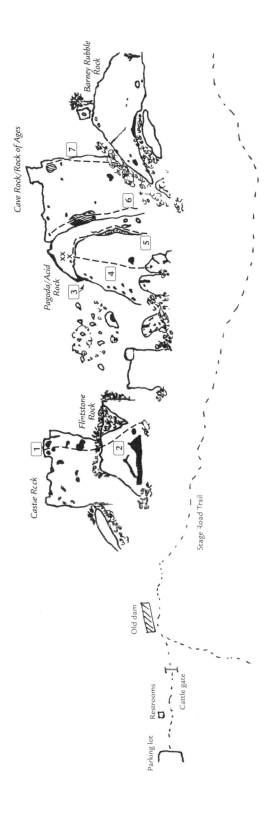

Castle Rock

Flintstone Rock

Pagoda/Acid Rock

Cave Rock/Rock of Ages

Barney Rubble Rock

Parking lot

Restrooms

Cattle gate

Old dam

Stage Road Trail

Approach: Park in the large lot at the entrance of Castle Rock Regional Park. As you head down the paved road into the park you will pass a swimming pool, dunk tanks, and restrooms. This becomes Stage Road, an old road used by folks to get to the summit of Mount Diablo. Follow Stage Road to a fork. Take the right fork passing through a cattle gate. Continue on the dirt trail, passing an old dam on your left side.

As you walk along, you will notice several large sandstone formations on the left side of the trail. Manzanita grows thick in certain sections, and poison oak is always within reach. Small windy foot trails meander from the main trail to various formations. It is a good idea to use the Castle Rock formation as a point of reference when looking for the rocks because it is easy to recognize.

Castle Rock

1. **Castle Rock Cave 5.6 ★★★** Nice toprope route. Gives the climber exposure and a spectacular view. Easy to set toprope. Use sandstone formations for girth-hitching.

Flintstone Rock

2. **Yabba Dabba Dudes 5.10a ★★★★** Seven bolts to one-bolt anchor. Walk off. This climb is a little runout before the first bolt. Lots of sandy pockets, which are slopey enough to keep you on your toes. 80 feet.

Castle Rock and Flintstone Rock, Pine Canyon

Jim Cope leading his way up Yabba Dabba Dudes, *Flintstone Rock*

Pagoda Rock and Rock of Ages, Pine Canyon

Pagoda Rock (a.k.a. Acid Rock)

The definition of pagoda is a sacred Buddist temple built as a memorial or shrine.

3. **Northwest Face 5.10a** ★ Three bolts to a three-bolt anchor. This short route begins inside of a cave and leads you out and up to the top. Usually climbed to set up top ropes for other climbs.

4. **Face 5.9** You need to rappel down to the anchors to toprope this route. Flakey, crumbly rock. 80 feet.

5. **The Pillar 5.8** ★ Several manky bolts to a three-bolt anchor. This route has a decent amount of bolts. Some bolts are good—three on the upper half of the route and two of the anchor bolts—but the remainder are very, very old . . . and scary. 120 feet.

Rock of Ages (a.k.a. Cave Rock)

6. **Rock of Ages Cave 5.9** ★★ Seven bolts. This route reaches 140 feet. Mediocre climbing to a stellar view. Heads up into the cave, then winds up and to the left.

7. **Bad Bolts 5.9** This route has twelve bolts that appear to have been here a very long time and have seen better days. This route is not recommended and could potentially be very dangerous.

Rock of Ages Cave, Pine Canyon

Nick Fain between a rock and a hard place on The Cleavage, *Indian Joe Caves*

INDIAN JOE CAVES

Located in the Sunol Regional Wilderness, Indian Joe Caves offers a multitude of climbing and bouldering possibilities. More than twenty toprope routes have been established, ranging from 5.3 to 5.12c. The highest formation reaches almost 40 feet. Many of these routes are longing to be bolted.

The wilderness area is the old site of an Ohlone Indian village. According to artifacts found here, the Ohlone subsisted primarily on acorns. Although exact dates are unknown, old records claim that the Geary family homesteaded the land now known as Sunol Regional Wilderness from the late 1800s through the beginning of the 1900s. On this land they had a house and a faithful employee named Joe Wilson. Joe, an Ohlone, was referred to by the Geary family as "Indian Joe." Joe was known as a "colorful" man with a great deal of exuberance. He lived in a small cabin with his family near the basalt rocks.

In 1959, the land, which covers 6,858 acres, was bought from a man named Willis Brinker and became an East Bay regional park by the year 1962. The park currently receives between 200,000 to 225,000 visitors per year.

Because the location is still not a popular crag by any means, it is doubtful you will ever find more than a handful of climbers here. Three main things deter most climbers from this spot: the short length of many routes, the fairly long (though gradual and pleasant) approach, and the lack of bolts. Although some routes are indeed short, they are fairly good quality, technical routes with equal amounts of balance, edging, and smearing required.

Southfacing view of Indian Joe Caves

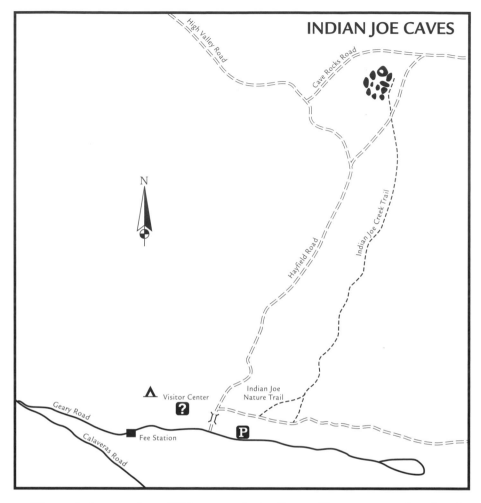

The park is open from 7:00 A.M. to dusk all year. The gates are closed and locked at night, so when the sun goes down, hustle back to your car unless you want to risk camping out.

Area Geology: For geologists, Indian Joe Caves is still a place of discovery with many unanswered questions. We do know that a fault most likely runs along Indian Joe Creek. Ophiolite (Greek for snake, snake-like strings, or bands of rock) was evident in the fault that created the rock types. Recent faulting associated with the San Andreas system sliced and diced the rock from the once snake-like bands to its current blob-like state.

The rocks were faulted onto the continent 100 to 120 million years ago. This rock in geological terms is very old. At least three different types of rock comprise a mélange here. The largest boulders are meta-basalts. If a rock type is classified as 'meta,' its current state was formed close to the earth's surface rather than deep inside the earth's core.

Large chunks of serpentinite surround the main rocks. Serpentine is a mineral, while serpentinite is a rock comprised solely of serpentine. These are mantle rocks, meaning they were formed beneath the earth's crust, lower than most other rock. When thinking of the earth's mantle, we can compare the earth to an apple. The crust of the earth is 10 kilometers thick. In relation to an apple, the crust is like an apple's skin. The mantle is everything from the base of the crust to the core of the earth, anywhere between 10 kilometers to 3,000 kilometers below the earth's surface.

There is also a significant amount of chert at Indian Joe Caves. Chert is a hard, dense sedimentary rock mostly made up of micro-crystalline quartz. Micro meaning the crystals are 30 microns or smaller. A micron is one-thousandth of a millimeter. The chert was deposited on the sea floor when this batch of rocks was formed.

TRIP INFORMATION

Climbing Season: Since Sunol Regional Park is located inland from the Bay, it is safe to say that summers are often sweltering. Between the months of June and August, climbing is best before noon or in the late afternoon. The average high temperature between the months of June and August is 87 degrees; but due to the cave-like features of the rock, certain climbs are always in the shade.

Autumn and spring offer the highest amount of fair weather climb time. The average high temperature here in winter is 55 degrees, and winter climbing is possible.

Fees: The day-use parking fee for Sunol Regional Park is $4.00.

Camping: Camping is available by reservation at Sunol Regional Park. Sites are $11 per night, which includes the park entrance fee. There are three group sites next to the visitor center, and you can reserve several different remote back-packing sites. For reservations, call (510) 636-1684. No showers are available at the park.

Dogs: Dogs are allowed on leashes near parking lots, campsites, or other developed areas. Dogs may be off-leash in open space and undeveloped areas with the exception of any wetland or marsh.

Emergency Services: Washington Hospital in Fremont, 11.5 miles away, is the closest medical care facility to Indian Joe Caves. The address is 2000 Mowry Avenue. The general phone number at the hospital is (510) 797-1111. From Interstate 680 at Calaveras, get back on I-680 heading southbound. Continue south, exiting at Mission Boulevard. Turn right on Mission and continue west until you get to Mowry Avenue. Here you will need to turn left. Drive less than 2 miles; the hospital will be on your left at the corner of Civic Center Drive.

Water Sources: There are water fountains at the visitor center, the campsites, and the parking area at Alameda Grove.

Telephones: A pay phone is located on the side wall of the interpretive center next to the visitor center.

Restrooms: There are outhouses near the visitor center and the parking areas.

Coffee Shops: The closest coffee spot to the crag is Sunol Coffeehouse & Café, located at 11882 Main Street. The cafe offers good espresso and coffee drinks, as well as a limited menu (not a choice establishment for vegetarians). From I-680 and California 84, exit at Calaveras and head west on CA 84 for less than a mile. Turn right onto Main Street, which leads you through the town of Sunol.

Markets: Sunol Market is within minutes of the park. From I-680 and Calaveras Road, head west on Calaveras (CA 84/Niles Canyon Road). Go less than a mile and turn right onto Main Street. Sunol Market is at 11984 Main Street in the town of Sunol.

Brewpubs: Bosco's Bones and Brew is also only minutes from Indian Joe Caves. Bosco's offers a full bar with a handful of beers on tap and a restaurant with a full menu. The dining is moderate to expensive, and the bar offers garlic fries and bruscetta in a casual western-style atmosphere. The pub is located in Sunol at 11922 Main Street. Drive west on Calaveras Road past I-680/Niles Canyon Road. Turn right onto Main Street and look for Bosco's on your left-hand side.

Gas Stations: There is a 76 located in downtown Pleasanton, 4.5 miles north of the Calaveras exit on I-680. Exit I-680 at Sunol Boulevard/Castlewood Drive. This is also the exit that leads to the Alameda County Fairgrounds. Drive east on Sunol Boulevard until you reach a fork in the road. Veer right onto First Street. Continue six blocks to Vineyard, where the station will be on your right.

Directions: Indian Joe Caves is roughly 40 miles from the Bay Bridge. The shortest route from San Francisco takes Interstate 80 (eastbound) to Interstate 580 (eastbound). Continue on I-580 until reaching I-680, where you will need to head south. Drive 8 miles and exit at CA 84/Calaveras Road. Turn left on Calaveras Road, go 4.1 miles to Geary Road, and turn left. Geary Road will enter the Sunol Regional Park within 1.5 miles.

Approach: From the parking areas near the interpretive center (50 yards past the fee station), cross the wooden bridge over a creek, and veer right, heading uphill on Hayfield Road. Hike 0.8 of a mile and look for a sign pointing to the right. This trail will lead you to Indian Joe Caves within 0.5 mile.

Indian Joe Creek Trail is another way to access the caves, but it is 0.2 mile longer than the other route. After crossing the bridge over the creek, turn right and follow the trail until you see Indian Joe Creek Trail on your left. Follow the winding trail uphill directly to the rocks. All of the routes are toproping problems, with the exception of *Bat Crack*.

1.   Bat Crack 5.5 ★★★ Access route to the bolts above.

2.   Roof 5.11b ★ Easy hike until you reach the awkward roof.

3.   The Ramp 5.7 ★

4.   Face 5.8 ★★

5.   The Cleavage 5.4 ★★★ Stem your way up the walls of these two large boulders.

6.   Face 5.9 ★★

7. Face 5.8 ★

8. Face 5.8 ★

9. Cote Memorial Wall 5.3 ★ Access line to set up toprope.

10. Face 5.11a ★★★

11. **Arête to Left Face 5.12c ★★★** Head halfway up the arête and then move out left onto a slightly overhanging, nearly featureless face.

12. On the Edge 5.10d ★★★

13. Grin and Bear It 5.10b ★★★

14. Face It 5.10c ★★★

15. Pull Up 5.10a ★★

16. Freeway 5.6 ★

17. **Orange Arête 5.11a ★★** Big move near the top.

18. **Little Eiger 5.12c ★★** Head left and up to a featureless crux, three-fourths of the way up the climb.

19. **Hour Glass 5.6 ★★** The toprope needs to be tossed through the hour-glass-like chimney formation from above where the two rocks meet.

20. **Yellow Brick Road 5.11a ★** Very short and slabby.

21. No Hands 5.10a ★

INDIAN JOE CAVES

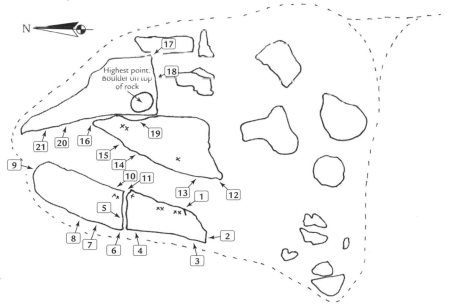

Leeta Steenwyck making her way up slick surfaces on Beaver Street Wall

BEAVER STREET WALL

Who would have guessed that in the heart of San Francisco, amid skyscrapers and cable cars, it is possible to find enjoyable outdoor rock climbing. At Beaver Street, a slick 45-foot wall is located just above the Castro neighborhood and offers routes ranging from 5.8 to 5.12. If the wall, which stretches end-to-end just over 100 feet, did not feature a prominent crack system directly up its center, few people would climb here, because of the difficulty of most lines. The incredibly hard rock is as smooth as glass in places, making the use of tiny chips and footless bulges a necessity in order to reach the anchors.

Chains are located directly above the main crack at the center of the wall. They are attached to a chain-link fence post, which is 2 inches in diameter and secured in a cement block. To reach the chains, either traditionally lead the main crack or climb up the 5.2 edge at the Beaver Street side of the wall located at the sidewalk. Climb past a tree and follow a narrow footpath to the chains midway on the wall.

Area Geology: Rock hounds love this place. The wall is radiolarian chert of the franciscan complex, similar to that of another San Francisco climbing location, Glen Canyon. The radiolarian material here was formed by the accumulation of microscopic plankton shells over the course of some 20 million years. Beaver Street Wall was formed during the Cretaceous period, anywhere from 65 to 140 million years ago. The wall is actually an old fault surface; a rare find in a densely populated city. It is slick in most areas because the fault surfaces polished themselves when the two sides ground past each other. Where is the northern side of the fault block? It was removed in order to build the park and a home on the north side of the park. Oxidized iron in the rock has left red streaks on the wall. According to geologists, the fault is "probably" no longer active.

TRIP INFORMATION

Climbing Season: Ask about weather in the "City by the Bay" and nearly all native San Franciscans will recite a quote oft attributed to Mark Twain (although there is no solid evidence of him ever having said it). No matter, "The coldest winter I ever spent was a summer in San Francisco" is still a memorable adage that rings true throughout most of the summer. Cool, foggy days are common, even in mid-July. Beaver Street is often warmest during the late summer and into the fall season. Sunny, yet crisp, days in November and often into early December are common and make for superb climbing conditions. Spring is a mixed bag. There are many beautiful sunny days in the rest of the Bay Area, while chilly San Francisco sits in fog. The wall's smooth surface requires dry conditions, so a thick layer of fog may limit the climbing for all but the most ardent diehards who do not want to leave the city.

Fees: Beaver Street Wall lies within the boundaries of what the San Francisco Parks and Recreation Department refers to as a public "mini-park" with no fees.

Camping: If you venture to the wall at night, you may notice people "camping" here, but they are generally homeless. To pitch a tent legally, head to the East Bay or drive north to the Marin Headlands. Kirby Camp is located on the north side of the Golden Gate Bridge off Conzelman Road. Reservations are required; call (415) 331–1540. Camping is available in the Berkeley hills at Tilden Regional Park. For information call (510) 562–PARK.

Dogs: There are no restrictions on dogs at Beaver Street Wall.

Emergency Services: Kaiser Permanente Medical Center is only 1.3 miles from Beaver Street Wall. It is located at 2241 Geary Boulevard between Baker Street and Lyon Street. The phone number is (415) 202–2000.

Water Sources: There are no water fountains at the wall. A liquor store is within walking distance on the corner of Castro Street and Fifteenth Street.

Telephones: The closest pay phone is also on the corner of Castro Street and Fifteenth Street in front of the little liquor store.

Restrooms: The park does not have restrooms. Unfortunately, a small wooded area just west of the wall behind a short fence is littered with toilet paper and reeks of urine. Watch where you step! The cafes and restaurants along Market Street offer the nearest legal relief.

Coffee Shops: There are several options for great coffee nearby. On the corner of Market Street and Noe Street is Café Flore. This coffee house serves strong brew and has great salads, sandwiches, pastries, and pastas. Outdoor seating is available. Peet's is across the street on Market; 0.5 block east of Noe.

Markets: A very large and very busy Safeway is only blocks away on Market Street at Church Street.

Brewpubs: Thirsty Bear Brewing Company and Gorden Biersch are not far away, but they are not exactly the choice watering hole for climbers (pricey, not to mention crowded). And who wants Vanilla Beer anyway? A better option, closer to Beaver Street and serving a much more eclectic clientele, is Zeitgeist. Although Zeitgeist does not brew its own beer, it does have anywhere between twenty and twenty-five fine beers on tap at all times. If you are a little dirty from climbing all day, you can feel comfortable hanging out at Zeitgeist. This bar is filled with bike messengers, motorcyclists, and otherwise laid-back individuals. A great outdoor patio is available, and a BBQ takes place on Sundays. Greasy food is served during limited hours on weekends. Zeitgeist is located on Valencia Street at the corner of Duboce Street. From Beaver Street, head down to Market Street and turn left. Turn right onto Valencia and go 3 blocks. Zeitgeist is on your left-hand side.

Gas Stations: A Chevron is located at 2399 Market Street near Castro Street and less than 1 mile from Beaver Street.

Directions: From Market Street and Van Ness Avenue in downtown San Francisco, head southwest on Market. Make a right turn on Noe Street, and an immediate left on Beaver Street. Drive up the hill. When the street curves to the right, look for a parking space. The Corona Heights Playground will be on your left, where the wall is in view.

Elizabeth Sheehan stepping carefully on Beaver Street Wall

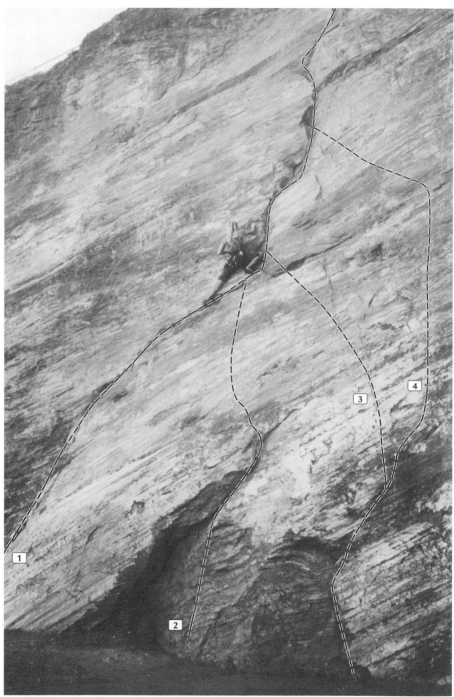

Beaver Street Wall

BEAVER STREET WALL

1. **5.10a ★★★** Follow the crack right and up. The crux of the climb is 15 feet off the deck. The second half of the climb holds a 5.8 rating.

2. **5.9 ★★** The easiest route to the top. Keep your eye out for nice crimps near the base.

3. **5.10d ★★★** Challenging climbing with slow, cat-like moves needed.

4. **5.11b ★★★** If the sun is shining on this section of rock and your fingertips are sweaty, this line is going to be a workout. Any feature or hairline crack within reach is needed to ascend the first 25 feet of this route.

Geologist Rick Ford pulling down at Glen Canyon

GLEN CANYON

Nestled amidst high-priced real estate within the boundaries of the "City by the Bay," there is actually some great bouldering and toproping. One of these gems is Glen Canyon in the Diamond Heights area, just a skip away from the downtown city hustle and bustle. Glen Park, where the canyon is located, is rarely (if ever) crowded, and parking (usually a nightmare in most of the city) is seldom an issue. David Brower and friends at the Sierra Club climbed here as early as 1930. The rock ranges from layered bands of jasperized chert with friendly jugs to finely polished sections to which even an insect would have a hard time sticking. The walls reach up to 20 feet and topropes are often set over a few problems with bad landings. With an abundance of bomber holds at the main rock band, many eliminate problems are set by the locals. Most landings are decent, but a crash pad will help on higher and more difficult problems.

A couple of bolts have been placed over a frequented highball bouldering problem called *The Unnatural Act* (Old Timers may know it as *Gunks Revisited*). Different variations exist ranging from 5.10 to 5.11. The outcropping is just uphill from the main rock band off the right of the trail. The Unnatural Act features an interesting roof problem with a better-than-average landing, although at close to 20 feet high, the bolts are much appreciated. To the right of this problem, a polished hand crack awaits, which goes at 5.8 if you avoid the majority of the face holds surrounding the crack.

Several outcroppings of rock exist other than the main rock band and The Unnatural Act area. On the walk to the crag, you will notice several large boulders

Main Area, Glen Canyon Boulders

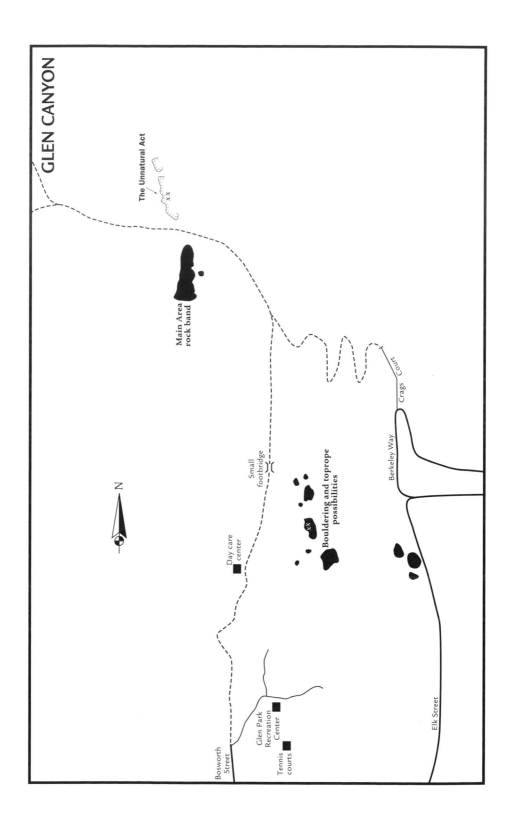

GLEN CANYON

The Unnatural Act

Main Area
rock band

N

Small
footbridge

Day care
center

Bouldering and toprope
possibilities

Bosworth
Street

Glen Park
Recreation
Center

Tennis
courts

Berkeley Way

Crags Court

Elk Street

next to and above, the main trail. The rocks are about 20–25 feet high, and at least one has bolts above for toproping. The rock quality is poor, but still climbable.

The park sits on 66 acres. If the weather is uncooperative, you can always head to the Glen Park Recreation Center at the south side of the park and play basketball indoors, or warm your paws in front of the comforting steam heaters.

Area Geology: The rock at Glen Canyon consists of radiolarian cherts of the franciscan complex. Sound complicated? It is. The layers of rock, each close to an inch thick, were formed anywhere from 65 to 140 million years ago. It is estimated that the amount of time needed to "make" chert is about 2,500 to 25,000 years per inch of material. In other words, it takes somewhere between 100,000 to 1 million years to accumulate just a few feet of the rock we often take for granted.

Even more interesting is the process by which the rock was formed. Radiolaria are microscopic plankton that have shells made of silica. As plankton died, their shells rained down on the ocean floor. The chert is the accumulation of these silica shells over very lengthy periods of time. Red and green colors in the rock are due to trace amounts of iron that have undergone different degrees of oxidation. The layered beds of radiolarian chert were flat when they were deposited but were later folded into their present wavy state by the forces that pushed them up onto the surface and shaped the San Francisco Peninsula.

TRIP INFORMATION

Climbing Season: Mild temperatures in San Francisco often allow climbing throughout the year in Glen Canyon. Although rarely too hot here, thick fog can make the rock slippery, and the chalk gooey, deterring even avid climbers. Fall is usually the best season, with warm weather and blue skies common. Rain can put a damper on climbing at the canyon in the winter months, but the chert dries fairly quick, usually allowing climbing within a day. It may not be wise to count on complete accuracy from San Francisco weather forecasters. Bay Area weather is often a guessing game from day to day.

Fees: No use fees or parking meters. (Caution! Some areas near the park have a sign posting a two-hour parking limit.)

Camping: You may notice people "camping" in the park, but they are most likely homeless. Camping is not permitted here. Drive north to the Marin Headlands or east into the Berkeley hills for camping options.

Kirby Camp is located in Marin County on the north side of the Golden Gate Bridge off Conzelman Road. Reservations are required. Call (415) 331–1540. Camping is available in Berkeley at Tilden Regional Park. For information, call (510) 562–PARK.

Dogs: Dogs are allowed inside the boundaries of Glen park if they are leashed.

Emergency Services: Several hospitals are nearby. Laguna Honda Hospital is the closest. It is only 0.5 mile from the park and located at 375 La Honda Boulevard. The phone number is (415) 664–1580. Drive out of the park south from Oshaughnessy, turn left on Portola Avenue, and then veer onto Woodside

The Unnatural Act, *Glen Canyon*

Avenue. Go 0.4 mile and turn right on La Honda Boulevard. San Francisco General is located at 1001 Potrero Avenue and Twenty-second Street. The phone number is (415) 206–8000. Another hospital in close proximity is Kaiser, located at 2425 Geary Boulevard. The phone is (415) 202–2000.

Water Sources: There are water fountains inside and outside of Glen Park Recreation Center.

Telephones: A pay phone is located inside Glen Park Recreation Center. The building is open Monday through Friday from 9:00 A.M. to 10:00 P.M., Saturday from 9:00 A.M. to 6:00 P.M., and Sunday from 11:00 A.M. and 5:00 P.M.

Restrooms: Restrooms are also located inside Glen Park Recreation Center.

Coffee Shops: Java City Bakery and Café is located at 5214 Diamond Heights Boulevard, 3.5 miles from the park.

Markets: A Safeway resides at 5290 Diamond Heights Boulevard near Java City. The cross street is Portola Drive.

Brewpubs: If you love a wide variety of beer the Toronado in San Francisco is the place to be. The hip pub in a very hippy section of the city has more than forty beers on tap in addition to at least fifty different types of Belgian brews. The location on Haight Street at Steiner Street is easy to get to from Glen Canyon. Parking in this section of the city is usually a frustrating experience (to say the least).

From Oshaughnessy Boulevard drive uphill to Portola Drive and turn right. Portola becomes Market Street. Follow Market to Castro Street and turn left. Drive roughly 8 blocks and turn right onto Haight Street. The address is 547 Haight Street.

Gas Stations: A gas station is only 0.5 mile from the park. It is at 701 Portola Drive and Oshaughnessy Boulevard. Leave the park on Bosworth Street, turn right onto Oshaughnessy, and drive a couple of blocks up the hill.

Directions: From downtown San Francisco, head west on Market Street toward Twin Peaks. Market will turn into Portola Drive. Go one block on Portola and turn left onto Oshaughnessy Boulevard. Follow Oshaughnessy downhill, making your first left onto Bosworth Street. Park here at the edge of the park.

Another popular route is to head south on Dolores Street from Market Street. Turn right on Duncan Street. Go 7 blocks and turn left on Diamond Heights Boulevard. Continue for 0.75 mile and turn right on Berkeley Way. You will see one outcropping on your left. For the main rock band, continue on Berkeley Way past this rock, turning left on Crags Court. At the end of the street, a trail will lead you down the hillside and the main rock band will be ahead and to your right. Parking is available on Berkeley Way and Crags Court, or at the south end of the park near the trailhead west of Glen Park Recreation Center.

Unknown Boulderer at The Magoos, Castle Rock State Park

South Bay Areas

CASTLE ROCK STATE PARK

Pulling on the sandstone at Castle Rock State Park has become a staple in the diet of many South Bay climbers. Bouldering has skyrocketed in popularity in the past decade, and many who frequent the crags claim the quality and quantity of bouldering here far exceed what you'll find on the climbs. In addition, some boulderers proclaim that Castle Rock sandstone is just as mighty as the famous rock at France's Fontainebleau.

Castle Rock State Park, located on the highest ridge of the Santa Cruz Mountains, encompasses more than 3,800 acres, and elevations range from 960 to 3,820 feet. The feature Castle Rock is at an elevation of 3,214 feet. Wildlife is abundant inside the park boundaries, especially at the higher elevations. There are black-tailed deer, gray fox, raccoon, California Mountain Kingsnake, Pacific Rattlesnake, mountain lion, and the endangered Marbled Murrelet.

There are over a dozen climbing and bouldering spots at Castle Rock State Park and more crags at nearby areas (Long Ridge Open Space Preserve, Saratoga Gap Open Space Preserve, Skyline Ridge Open Space Preserve, and the Upper Stevens Creek Open Space Preserve) for a total of at least 260 established toprope, sport, and traditional routes. Out of all these areas, five hold the choicest and most popular routes. These areas are inside the boundaries of Castle Rock State Park and Sanborn County Park and are the only areas covered in this guide. Some popular bouldering areas are marked on the overview map and briefly mentioned in this section, but due to the vast number of potential bouldering problems (several hundred possibilities), a more detailed description is beyond the scope of this guide.

More descriptions are available in the *Rock Climber's Guide to Skyline Boulevard* written by Bruce Morris and published by Morcomm Press. This book is available at Shoreline Mountain Products in San Rafael and other outdoor shops.

Area Geology: The uniquely shaped sandstone, with its caves, pockets, and bulbous features, is probably the main attraction for tourists, hikers, and of course, climbers at Castle Rock State Park. The sandstone, known as Vaqueros sandstone, has pockets and caves called tafoni carved out of it. In addition to the tafoni, the sandstone has honeycombed features, or fretwork, as well as large round spheres sticking out from the rock, what geologists refer to as cannonballs.

Over time, erosion has exposed the outer surface of the rock, which changes slowly due to weather factors such as rain and wind. The area is in an active fault zone. The epicenter of the 1989 Loma Prieta Earthquake, a 7.2 on the richter scale, was not far from here, and the San Andreas Fault divides the Los Trancos Open Space Preserve, only 9 miles to the north.

The interesting shapes and formations of rock, along with the lush vegetation, make the park appear to be something out of a fairy tale.

TRIP INFORMATION

Climbing Season: Fall and spring are generally the best seasons to climb here, unless you are lucky enough to encounter a dry spell in winter, or cooler than average temperatures in summer. Much of the bouldering requires open hands on slopers, making sweaty palms on hot days a huge bummer. Crisp, dry days in winter are often perfect conditions for bouldering at Castle Rock State Park.

When there is heat at Castle Rock, there are bugs. Be sure to carry bug repellent with you, especially between April and September. Mosquitoes and evil little yellow flies may drive you batty at the park if you do not come prepared. Most bug repellents keep the mosquitoes away quite well, but the biting yellow flies, especially prevalent at Indian Rock and Summit Rock, often require superstrong chemicals, such as those containing DEET, to keep them away.

Rain in the wintertime is taxing on sandstone. After a good rain, it is best to wait at least two full days for the sandstone to dry out thoroughly. Crucial holds can break off easily if under strain when soggy.

Summit Rock, Indian Rock, and Castle Rock can be damp and cool in the winter months. For warmer climbing head for Goat Rock, which faces south and is much sunnier. The majority of the routes at Castle Rock Falls are shaded throughout the day, but a few (such as the popular Falls Route) are often drenched in sun.

Fees: At Castle Rock State Park, day-use parking fees are $2.00, although parking is usually available alongside Skyline Boulevard/California Highway 35 near the park entrance. The pullout for Indian Rock and the parking lot for Summit Rock are inside the boundaries of Sanborn County Park, where there are no fees.

Camping: There is a hike-in campground inside the boundaries of Castle Rock State Park, but most people don't want to hike after climbing all day. The sites are located 2.8 miles from the main parking lot, which requires at least an hour walk on the Saratoga Gap Trail.

If you are not up for the hike, you can take the uninteresting route and walk north on CA 35 from the main parking lot for less than 1 mile to the entrance to Los Altos Rod and Gun Club. Take the dirt service road on the left that heads downhill for 1 mile to the campground. This hike is a mile shorter than the trail. Be sure to take the service road and not the road that leads onto the property of the gun club.

Twenty-five sites are available primarily on a first-come, first-served basis, but a few sites can be reserved. Water and an outhouse are available at the campground, and a fee of $5.00 per site must be paid at the ranger station in the main parking lot. To reserve a site at Trail Camp, call (831) 338–8861.

Saratoga Springs Campground is on CA 9 heading south before the city of Saratoga. Don't waste your time or money here. The campground is littered, the port-a-potties are dirty, and campsites are more than $20 per night.

A better alternative is Big Basin State Park, 15.9 miles southwest of Castle Rock. It takes roughly thirty-five minutes to drive to Big Basin State Park from Castle Rock State Park. Here you can enjoy camping in a peaceful, clean setting. Four separate campgrounds and 146 campsites are available. Showers are also available at 25 cents for three minutes. Regular sites are $12.00 per night, with a fee of $3.00 for each additional vehicle per night. Tent cabins are also available. Reservations are recommended for camping at Big Basin, California's oldest state park, but weekday visitors (holidays excluded) usually have plenty of sites to choose from. Call (800) 444-PARK or (408) 338-8860, for more information.

To reach the park from Castle Rock, head north on CA 35 and turn left (west) onto CA 9. Drive 5.7 miles and make a right onto California 236/Big Basin Way. Continue for 7.7 winding miles into the park. The address is 21600 Big Basin Way in Boulder Creek.

Dogs: Dogs are not allowed at Castle Rock State Park. Sanborn County Park does allow dogs if they are on leash, so taking your dog to either Summit Rock or Indian Rock is acceptable.

Emergency Services: Community Hospital is in Los Gatos, 4.6 miles from Saratoga at 815 Pollard Road. From Big Basin Way/CA 9, veer right onto Saratoga Avenue. Go 1.3 miles and turn right on Fruitvale Avenue. Turn left on Allendale Avenue and right onto Quito Road. Turn left onto Pollard Road and drive 1.4 miles to Community Hospital. The phone number is (408) 378-6131.

Water Sources: The only water in the park is located at Castle Rock's Trail Camp. BYOW.

Telephones: A pay phone is located near the entrance of the main parking lot and also at Trail Camp.

Restrooms: An outhouse is located in the main parking lot and off the main trail leading from the main parking lot to Castle Rock. Trail Camp has out houses as well.

Coffee Shops: International Coffee Exchange is located in Saratoga on Big Basin Way at Third Street across the street from Bank of America. The coffee is good and light fare is available, such as pastries, sandwiches, and juices.

Markets: A Safeway is located at 12876 Saratoga/Sunnyvale Road in Saratoga.

Brewpubs: The sleepy little town of Saratoga does not have a brewpub, but there is a local bar that isn't a bad spot to stop for a beer after climbing all day. The downside of this pub, The Bank, is the fact that it does not have food. The Bank is located on Big Basin Way between Saratoga-Los Gatos Road and Third Street.

Brittania Arms of Almaden is located at 5027 Almaden Expressway at Cherry Avenue in San Jose only 3 miles from Saratoga proper. There are more than fifteen beers on tap, including some favorites of our neighbors across the pond. John Courage, Bass, and of course, Guiness. Typically greasy bar food is available, and several TVs play the current football, basketball, or hockey games. Rowdy sports fans are often sucking down beers here; so if you desire peace and quiet this is not the place to be.

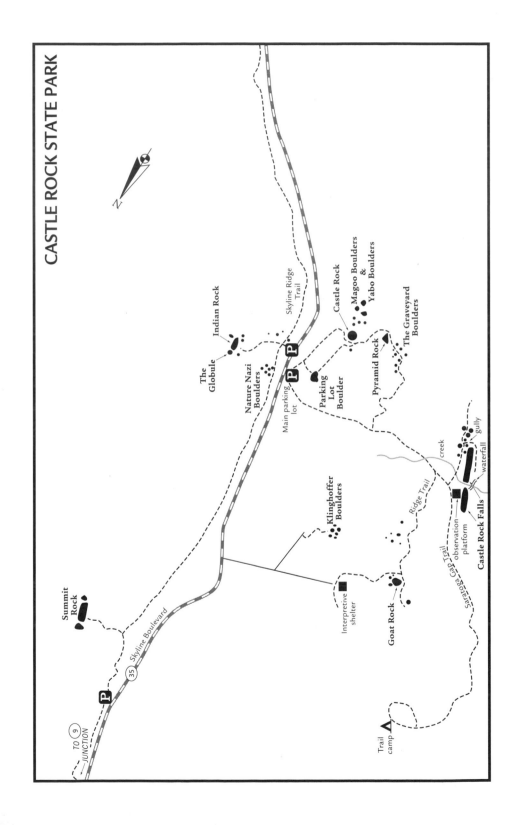

CASTLE ROCK STATE PARK

N

TO 9
JUNCTION

35

Skyline Boulevard

P

Summit
Rock

Skyline Ridge
Trail

The
Globule   Indian Rock

Nature Nazi
Boulders

P
P

Main parking
lot

Castle Rock

Magoo Boulders
&
Yabo Boulders

Parking
Lot Boulder

Pyramid Rock

The Graveyard
Boulders

Klinghoffer
Boulders

Interpretive
shelter

Goat Rock

Ridge Trail

Saratoga Gap Trail

observation
platform

Castle Rock Falls

creek

waterfall

gully

Trail
camp

Gas Stations: A Unocal 76 is located in Saratoga on the corner of Big Basin Way/CA 9 and Saratoga/Sunnyvale Road.

Directions: From San Francisco, head south on Interstate 280 toward San Jose. Exit onto Interstate 85 (southbound) toward Gilroy and exit at De-Anza Boulevard. Make a right on De-Anza, which becomes Saratoga/Sunnyvale Road. Turn right at CA 9/Big Basin Way and continue uphill on a curvy two-lane road for 6 miles. At the crest of the hill turn left. This is CA 35 (heading south). The main parking lot at Castle Rock is 2.5 miles from the junction of CA 9 and CA 35.

CASTLE ROCK

Castle Rock provides climbers with a dozen established toproping routes that reach as high as 50 feet. These range from 5.6 to 5.12, plus the 5.4 line used to set up topropes. A heavy-duty belay pole, which is cemented into the top of the rock, is suitable for toproping and rappelling. To reach the belay pole, climb the 5.4 line to the left of the cave on the east side of the rock. Although only a couple of the routes are considered high quality, the area is still very popular due to the vast numbers of fine boulders around Castle Rock and in the nearby vicinity.

West Face

All these lines are toprope routes except *Chockstone*.

1. Roof 5.10a ★

2. Unknown 5.12 ★ Climb the first half of *Farewell* and then move out to the left and continue up.

3. Farewell to Arms 5.10a ★★★ A couple drop knees may help you on this climb as well as a fist jam, otherwise dynoing is an option.

4. Aeronautical Engineer 5.11b ★★★★ There are two cruxes on this climb. The first is an overhanging move away from the upper left edge of the cave, and the next is a weird mantle that gets you over a roof two-thirds of the way up the climb.

5. Roof 5.11+ This stiff roof climb begins on the right edge of the cave and heads up and over using small pockets and sloped edges.

6. Chockstone 5.8 ★★★ A good climb for learning to place protection. Nice huecos and big sloped holds offer plenty of options for ascension.

East Face

All these lines are toprope routes except *Summit Route*.

7. Summit Route 5.4 Safest way to get to the top to set topropes.

8. Mantle Groove 5.10c ★ Make your way up huecos and nice jugs, then "push" the cruxy mantle near the top.

9. Face 5.9 ★ Trust your feet. Plenty of rests.

10. Chimney 5.6 ★ Squeeze and scoot.

CASTLE ROCK, WEST FACE

5

6

Castle Rock, West Face

CASTLE ROCK, EAST FACE

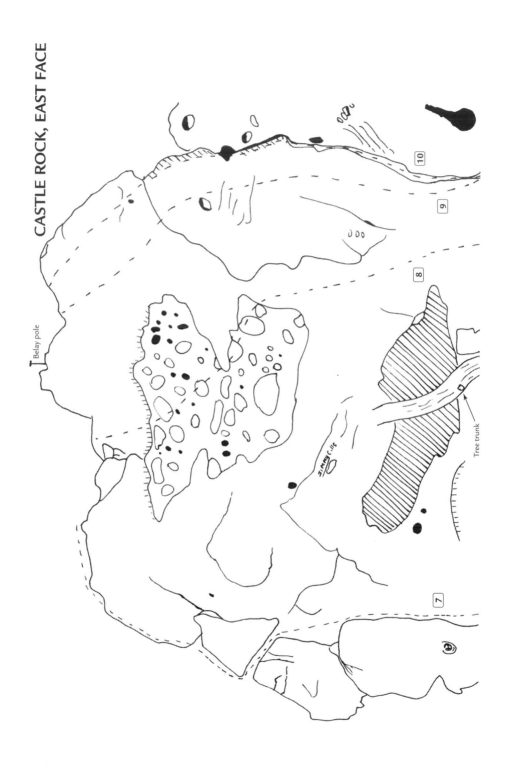

Belay pole

Tree trunk

7 8 9 10

Unknown climber on The Falls, Castle Rock Falls

CASTLE ROCK FALLS

The sandstone walls on both sides of Castle Rock Falls offer sporty climbs that reach up to 80 feet. The majority of the climbs are 5.11s and 5.12s, but a handful of easier routes are available, most requiring some gear placement. All of the climbs can be toproped due to the easy walk-off and placement of anchors. A gully on the far right side of the wall provides easy access to the tops of all climbs except *The Falls* (the only route on the left side of the waterfall). Either rappell down from the platform, or cross the creek at the top of the falls and follow a trail behind the cliffs and down a gully to the front of the climbs.

1. **The Falls 5.10a ★★★** Seven bolts to the base of the waterfall observation platform, which is used for an anchor. This route is by far the most popular route at Castle Rock Falls. Unfortunately, the crux is below the first bolt. A stick clip is helpful due to a potential ground fall of nearly 15 feet. After the first bolt, the climbing eases up in a big way with mainly 5.6 to 5.8 moves. The remaining bolts do meander a bit and are farther apart, but the lengthy climb (almost 100 feet) has a beautiful view. Be ready to be in the spotlight of tourists atop the platform.

2. **The Oracle 5.11a ★★★** Five bolts to a two-bolt anchor. Not only is this route thin and reachy, but it is also marked with a little moss for an extra challenge. Begin on the right side of the waterfall. After the third bolt you can either continue straight up and a little to the left, clipping two more bolts before reaching the anchors, or you can veer right (2a) clipping a bolt through a more difficult section and moving into *The Greeboo*.

3. **The Greeboo 5.10c R ★★** Four bolts to a two-bolt anchor shared with *The Oracle*. The first half of the climb is the climb. The remainder is runout 5.8 slab. Gear can be used in cracks to the right before reaching the fourth bolt.

4. **Charlie Solo 5.6 ★** Pro to 3.5″. A little dirty, especially near the top.

5. **Anti-Christ 5.11d ★★** Four bolts to a two-bolt anchor. Climb up a flake and clip the first bolt. After climbing past a bulging edge, head up and left following the right side of the arête to the top.

CASTLE ROCK FALLS, LEFT SIDE

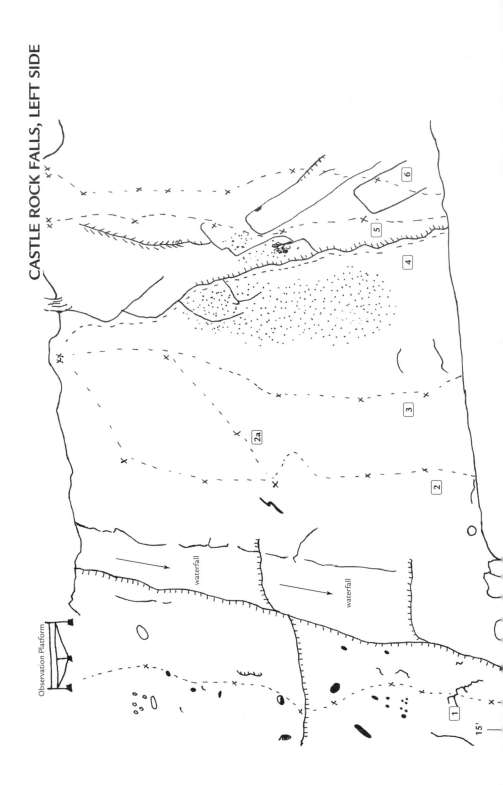

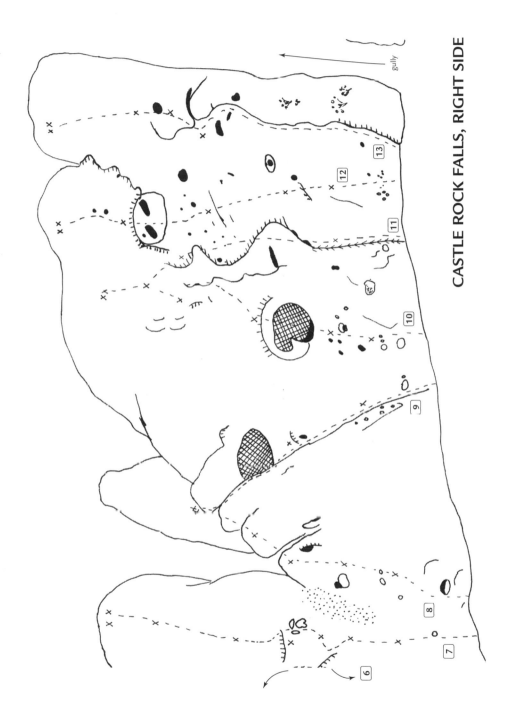

CASTLE ROCK FALLS, RIGHT SIDE

gully

Stewart Green on Putrefaction, *Castle Rock Falls*

6. **Above the Law 5.11d ★★★** Six bolts to a two-bolt anchor. Slab climb up the right side of the ramp and follow the bolts past a series of small bulges and flakes to the 5.11d crux, which is past the fifth bolt.

7. **Clamydia 5.11d ★★★★★** Six bolts to a two-bolt anchor. Challenging route with a good amount of slopers and fingery crimps. Tackle a slightly overhanging section between the second and third bolts, then be sure to save some strength for yanking up and over the "clams." Beta intensive.

8. **Cleotitis 5.12b ★★★** Four bolts to two-bolt anchor. Short, stiff, vertical route with minuscule holds. Start to the right of *Clamydia* and follow the white streak up the rock. Good smearing technique required.

9. **POS Crack 5.10c ★★** Mixed route with two bolts available for first 30 feet, then pro to 3.5" needed to the two-bolt anchor.

10. **Convulsions 5.11b ★★★** Mixed route with five bolts to a two-bolt anchor. Gear up to 2" can be used for the midsection where the difficulty eases and is mainly 5.9 climbing. Awkward reachy crux at second bolt.

11. **Leading to Death 5.9 ★★** Mixed route with three bolts to a two-bolt anchor shared with *Convulsions*. Pro to 3".

12. **Putrefaction 5.11a ★★★** Four bolts to two-bolt anchor. This line begins with 5.10 slab climbing that leads to a difficult roof requiring either super-mono pocket power or serious ingenuity to tackle.

13. **Degeneration 5.10a ★★** Mixed route with three bolts to a two-bolt anchor. The first half of the route is 5.7 climbing up a dihedral just to the left of the gully.

GOAT ROCK

Goat Rock is a popular climbing destination, partially due to an abundance of moderate routes, but also due to the sheer height of the rock, which reaches 80 feet. Good anchor bolts can be reached by climbing up the backside of the rock. (Although third class, this approach is exposed and airy.) Bring long slings unless you want your rope to get chewed up from the abrasive sandstone. This large rock, with its plentiful pockets and caves, has several routes, most with ratings below 5.10a. The right side of the rock offers several toprope variations from 5.5 to 5.9. All of the lines are toprope problems except *Left Side of Great Roof.*

1. **Lunge Route 5.11c ★** Reachy and footless.

2. **Triple Overhang 5.9 ★★** Tricky moves.

3. **Overhang Continuation 5.7 ★★** Takes the easy route to the left of the roof.

4. **Left Side of Great Roof 5.12a ★★** Three bolts to two-bolt anchor.

Goat Rock, Castle Rock State Park

5.   **The Great Roof 5.10b** ★★★ Tackles the roof and leaves you with a nice pump.

6.   **Various Face Routes 5.4-5.9** ★★ Good clean fun. There are four bolts on top of Goat Rock.

INDIAN ROCK

Indian Rock offers a little bit of everything: sporty overhanging routes, slab routes, cracks, and difficult lines with bulges and slopers. It gets a lot of visitors because it is located less than five minutes from the parking pullout. As is the case with most cliffs at Castle Rock State Park, a few high quality boulder problems are located right next to the climbing. All of the routes on the South Face can be toproped and walked off easily.

Several routes exist on Indian Rock, while the small formation on the north edge of it, called The Globule, holds four short 5.10s and 5.11s.

Unknown climber on Baby Fat, The Globule

Southwest Face

1.   Jail Bird 5.12a ★★★ Two bolts to two-bolt anchor. Follow the left edge of the rock past huecos on thin edges and pockets. For a harder variation, climb over the large hueco near the base and up left to the first bolt.

2.   South Face 5.9 ★ Two bolts to a two-bolt anchor. This face climb is just left of the tree. Low angle slab climbing with a huge rest after second bolt.

3.   Puckered Starfish 5.10a ★★★ Two bolts to two-bolt anchor. Follow a diagonal crack up and left, placing pro if needed, then clip the first bolt and pull through on crimps to the second bolt. Easy climbing between the second bolt and the top.

4.   Donkey Dong 5.11c ★★★★ Five bolts to two-bolt anchor. Climb up the overhanging arête on good jugs and pockets. Use the crimps on the left side of arête near the fourth bolt, or go big with a dyno near the top. Beware of the loose chunk of rock on the arête near the third bolt.

Northeast Face

5.   Viscious Circles 5.10c ★★★★ Four bolts to two-bolt anchor. Great line for practicing the fine art of commitral. Crux between first and second bolts.

6.   Blowing Bubbles 5.10a R ★★★ Two bolts to two-bolt anchor shared with *Viscious*. Lots of good huecos and pockets on this line. You can move to the left and clip the third bolt of *Viscious* if you do not wish to risk the 5.6 runout to the anchors.

7.   Dismal Abysmal 5.11c ★ Three bolts to two-bolt anchor. Do not fall before the first bolt! This 30-foot route heads left above the cave.

8.   Krokus 5.11d ★★★★ Three bolts to two-bolt anchor. You can use 3″ pro to protect the crack beneath the second bolt. Easy climbing to second bolt, then sustained and difficult moves required climbing up the arête to the anchors.

9.   Hocus 5.11b R ★ Two bolts to two-bolt anchor. Scary climb until you clip the second bolt. If you do not make the clip, the fall down and over the edge could turn ugly. Slab route with a shortage of holds.

Southwest Face, Indian Rock

Northeast Face of Indian Rock, left side

NORTHEAST FACE OF INDIAN ROCK, RIGHT SIDE

Tree   To The Globule

10.   **Strip Poker 5.12a ★★★** Five bolts to two-bolt anchor. Start on right edge of far right cave, climbing up and out over edge of the cave using the plethora of huecos and pockets. Continue up a slabby section and finally over a roof where the 5.12a section is below the anchors.

SUMMIT ROCK

The views of the Silicon Valley from Summit Rock make it party central for late night visitors. Unless a crackdown by park rangers is in the works, broken glass, beer cans, and other garbage will continue to detract from this otherwise fine area. The broken bottles are unsightly and dangerous. There are a total of twenty-seven routes, nearly all leadable. Five of these routes are cracks offering good protection. The highest climbs here reach nearly 70 feet, and only a handful of climbs are less than 30 feet. The most popular and choicest climbs, all at the Lower Tier, are the only routes covered in this chapter.

1.   **The Molar 5.11a ★★** Four bolts to two-bolt anchor. This route is located on the opposite side of the spire from *Spung-Lick-A-Litus*.

2.   **Spung-Lick-A-Litus 5.12b ★★** Five bolts to an anchor (cold shut and bolt). The crux of this route is cranking off the two-finger pocket at the base and managing to smear and crimp your way up and left to the arête.

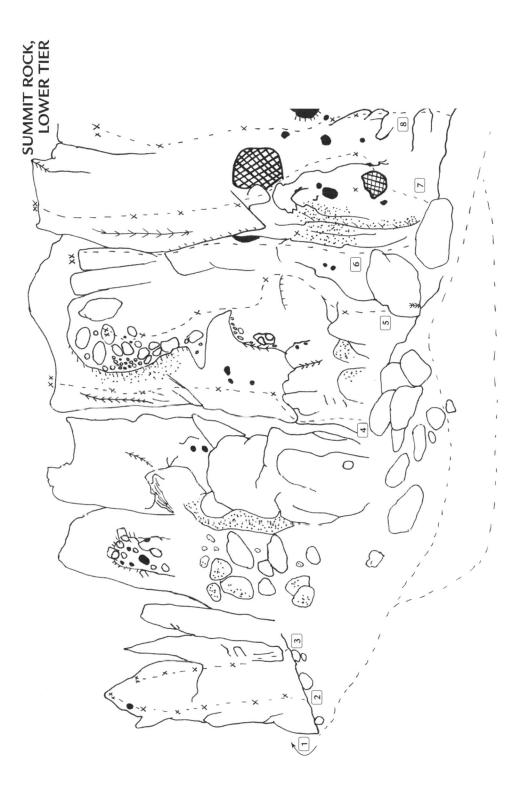

SUMMIT ROCK, LOWER TIER

Lower Tier of Summit Rock, left side

Tree Surgeon
5.9 crack
around corner

Lower Tier of Summit Rock, right side

Leeta Steenwyk

Richie Esquibel on University of Santa Clara Practice Climb #1, *Summit Rock*

3. **Worm Belly 5.10b ★★** Four bolts to a two-bolt anchor. Worm your way up this line using balance and edging techniques.

4. **Bolt Filcher 5.10d ★★★★** Four bolts to a two-bolt anchor. A serious high step, along with sloper smacking, pulls you through the crux just past the third bolt.

5. **University of Santa Clara Practice Climb #1 5.8 ★★★★★** Four bolts to two-bolt anchor. The first bolt on this climb won't keep you off the ground, so make sure you don't fall until the second bolt is clipped! Huge jugs and honeycomb holds take you on a fun ride to the anchors.

6. **Double Cracks 5.9 ★★** Pro to 3.5″. Lots of stemming and shouldery moves needed, along with some good jams.

7. **Rectalphobiac 5.11b ★★★★** Five bolts to a two-bolt anchor. Weird move at the first bolt, then easy runout climbing takes you to the difficult moves on the arête between the fourth and fifth bolts.

8. **Glob of Shit 5.10c ★★** Four bolts to two-bolt anchor. Overhanging but juggy. Not as "shitty" as you may expect!

9. **Chancroid 5.11c R** Three bolts to a two-bolt anchor. Difficult moves from the ground up to the third bolt, then runout easy climbing to the anchors.

10. **Skill Saw Gourmet 5.11d ★★★★★** Four bolts to two-bolt anchor with chain links. Very popular vertical climb with challenging crux after second bolt.

11. **Tree Surgeon 5.10a ★★★** Pro to 3.5″. A sawed-off tree trunk midway up in the crack marks this climb well. The crack appears to swallow climbers up in spots.

BOULDERING

Bouldering at Castle Rock State Park has become incredibly popular in the past few years. Many boulderers and climbers believe that the quality of bouldering problems exceeds the quality of climbing routes here. Whether or not this is true, the sheer number of boulders and problems far outweighs the number of climbs at and near Castle Rock State Park.

For the highest concentration of boulders, head up to Castle Rock where you will find several boulders surrounding Castle Rock proper. Several other bouldering areas are within a five-minute walk. Magoo, Yabo, and The Graveyard are only moments away.

Magoo and Yabo Boulders (behind the southeast side of Castle Rock) offer a huge variety of possibilities from slabby, smearing problems to sloped overhangs. These problems range in difficulty from V0 to V10. An area often referred to as The Graveyard has a dozen boulders lining either side of the trail that leads downhill and southwest of Castle Rock toward the falls. The Eco-Terrorist Boulder resides here with the incredibly difficult *Eco-Terrorist* V11 (some say V12)

Pyramid Rock, Castle Rock State Park

Billy Hamblin, from the flatlands of Florida, enjoying The Magoo Boulders at Castle Rock State Park

problem Chris Sharma sent in 1997. Only 25 yards south, the crimpy, beta-intensive *Domino Theory Traverse* (V4) awaits.

Just southeast of Castle Rock is Pyramid Rock. This striking 25-foot boulder just off the side of the trail has a juicy highball problem that follows a left-facing finger to hands crack to the top. Pads and/or spotters are recommended due to the bad landing over several potentially painful rocks.

The Parking Lot Boulder holds some of the choice problems in the park. It is also a favorite because of the short three-minute walk from the main parking lot. The boulder offers more than twenty-five quality problems spanning the range from V0 to V10. The notable *Yabo Roof* (V5), named after first ascentionist John Yablonski (1956–1991), is a desirable problem that comes out of the cave and tops out above it. To the right of it is another worthy problem called the *Coz Daddy Roof* (V6).

The Klinghoffer Boulders also provide a good deal of problems and are

Chris Summit on Eco-Terrorist Boulder, *V11/12*

Parking Lot Boulder, southeast corner, Castle Rock State Park

generally not as crowded on weekends as the boulders near Castle Rock. Two of these boulders have bolts on top for toproping the highball problems. There are several other boulders a short walk from the Klinghoffers along the Ridge Trail behind the east side of Goat Rock.

Finally the Nature Nazi Boulders rest beside the edge of the Skyline Ridge Trail near Indian Rock, which also has a handful of good boulders surrounding it.

SKYLINE BOULEVARD SLABS

If you like the thrill of a runout on nearly featureless slab, you will love Skyline Boulevard Slabs. This little crag is located only a few miles north of Castle Rock State Park inside the boundaries of the Skyline Ridge Open Space Preserve.

Weathered oaks and Douglas firs are abundant here amidst the grasslands and creeks. Emerald green moss-covered boulders rest in Peters Creek, where a noisy waterfall stimulates another of the five senses. Coyotes, bobcats, the occasional mountain lion, and many banana slugs call this space home. The westward view from the tops of the slabs overlooking the canyon below give you an airy feeling of solitude, and the sunsets after a hard day of hiking and climbing are amazing!

Sandstone outcroppings are strewn about the landscape. For information on geology, as well as nearby amenities, take a look at the section on Castle Rock State Park. The main parking lot at Castle Rock on California 35 is just 5.6 miles south of the trailhead leading to Skyline Boulevard Slabs.

TRIP INFORMATION

Climbing Season: As is the case with all sandstone after a rain, the rock is very fragile in many spots. Crucial holds and dangerous sections of rock can break off quite easily, causing unsafe conditions, and worse yet, the destruction of otherwise beautiful lines. After a rain, allow the rock to dry for at least two full days to keep holds from breaking off. If conditions are damp or humid after a rain, it is possible the rock will remain fragile for more than two days.

Warm temperatures in the summer can make climbing taxing, with some of the sun-drenched routes hard for even the sand flies to stick to. If climbing in the heat, move with the shade. Most climbers find the rock more suitable in the spring and fall. Wintertime climbing can be excellent if a hat and fleece are in hand, but often it gets too cold.

Fees: There are no fees for hiking or climbing in the Skyline Ridge Open Space or Long Ridge Open Space Preserves, which is where the hike to the slabs starts.

Dogs: A permit is required for dogs in the Long Ridge Open Space Preserve. A box is located at Grizzly Flat Trailhead on the east side of CA 35. A form must be filled out and placed in the box. No fee is required and the permit is good for one day only. All dogs must be kept on leash.

Water Sources: No water fountains or spigots are available in either of the open space preserves. BYOW.

Telephones: No public phones are located at either of the open space preserves. There are emergency phones located along CA 35, but employees for the Midpeninsula Regional Open Space District claim many are inoperable.

Restrooms: Public restrooms are located at the parking lot in Skyline Ridge Open Space Preserve, 2.1 miles north of the pullout for Grizzly Flat on CA 35. From the intersection of California 9, travel 5.2 miles north on CA 35.

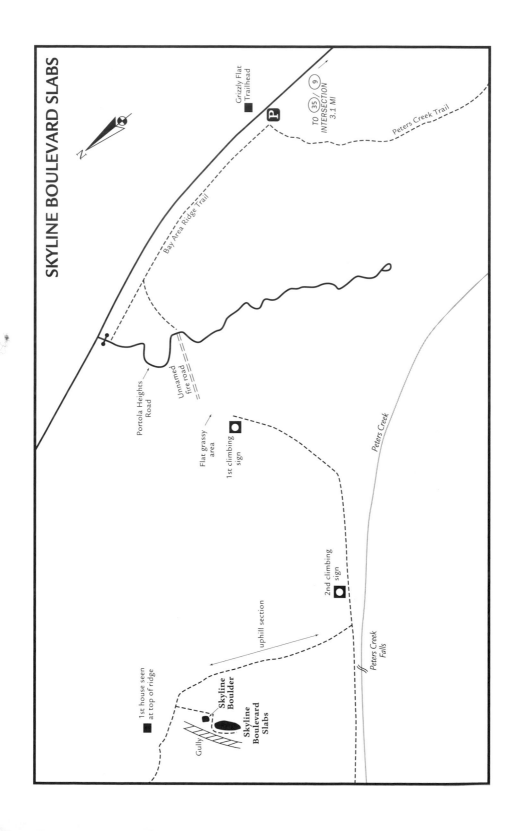

SKYLINE BOULEVARD SLABS

N

TO 35 / 9
INTERSECTION
3.1 MI

Peters Creek Trail

Grizzly Flat
Trailhead

P

Bay Area Ridge Trail

Portola Heights
Road

Unnamed
fire road

Flat grassy
area

1st climbing
sign

2nd climbing
sign

Peters Creek

Peters Creek
Falls

uphill section

1st house seen
at top of ridge

Skyline
Boulder

Skyline
Boulevard
Slabs

Gully

Directions: From San Francisco, head south on Interstate 280 toward San Jose. Exit onto Interstate 85 (southbound) and get off at De-Anza Boulevard. Make a right on De-Anza, which will become Saratoga/Sunnyvale Road. Turn right at California 9/Big Basin Way and continue uphill on CA 9. At the crest of the hill, turn right onto CA 35 heading northbound. Drive 3.1 miles to a parking pullout on the west side of the highway.

Approach: Although the slabs are inside the boundaries of the Skyline Ridge Open Space Preserve, the trail to the crag begins in the Long Ridge Open Space Preserve and heads north. From the parking pullout walk on the west side of the highway on the northbound dirt trail that runs parallel to CA 35. Go 0.5 mile down the trail and look for a narrow trail that leads to your left, heading west. If you come to the paved Portola Heights Road, you have gone about 0.2 mile too far and need to turn back to find the narrow foot trail that heads west.

Follow the foot trail down to the paved road (Portola Heights) and cross over it to an old fire road (often overgrown with weeds) on the opposite side. Portola Heights Road is off limits to hikers, but apparently it is okay to cross the road here to reach the continuing trails. Walk less than 0.25 mile northwest on the fire trail to a small open field. You will know you are in the right place if there is a square-shaped chunk of concrete in the middle of the space. Continue west through the small field and pick up the creek-bound trail. Head down and right past the first sign with climbing regulations. Follow the creek downstream for about 0.5 mile to the second sign with climbing regulations, which is placed on the right side of the trail. Continue past the sign for roughly 25 yards where the trail forks. Left continues along the creek, and up and right heads toward the slabs. If you reach the falls, you have gone too far.

Following the trail northeast, you will gain 900 feet of elevation before reaching the Skyline Boulevard Slabs. When you reach the top of the ridge, turn left before the first house you see, following a short trail that will lead you directly to Skyline Boulder and a gully that will lead you directly down (30 yards) to the slabs.

SKYLINE BOULEVARD SLABS

1. **Cranberries Variation 5.9** Five bolts to a two-bolt anchor.

2. **Cranberries 5.9 R ★** Three bolts to a two-bolt anchor. Too much moss and lichen detract from this otherwise good climb.

3. **Unknown 5.10 ★** Six bolts to a two-bolt anchor. Ditto above concerning moss and lichen. Climb right after the fifth bolt over a roof to the anchors on the right, or head to the left after fifth bolt for easier climbing.

4. **Unknown 5.10d R ★★★** Seven bolts to a two-bolt anchor. If you miss the second bolt, you will face a ground fall. The crux is just past the third bolt, where the rock beneath you lacks holds and trusting your feet on micro nubbins is necessary. After the fourth bolt, a friendly section of roof with good feet and fine jugs awaits you. Can be led to the left or right anchors after the sixth bolt.

SKYLINE BOULEVARD SLABS

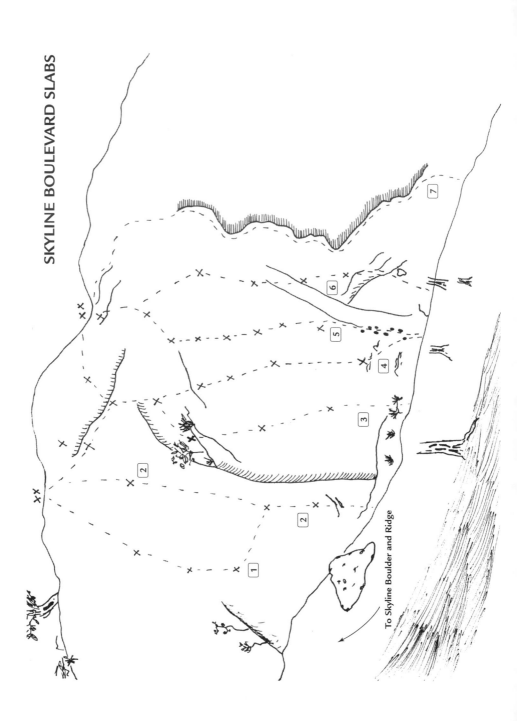

To Skyline Boulder and Ridge

Barbara Smejkal on Old Bolt Ladder, *Skyline Boulevard Slabs*

5.   Old Bolt Ladder 5.10c/d ★★★★ Eight bolts to a two-bolt anchor. This climb is a little runout to the first bolt, which is not exactly bomber. The rusty old bolt seems solid but is protruding a bit from the rock. Thank goodness for the healthy second bolt directly beneath the crux because the move requires either arms the length of Manute Bol's, or very good slab technique.

6.   Unknown 5.8/5.10b ★★★ Five bolts to a two-bolt anchor. The variance in the difficulty rating depends on whether or not you use the tree, which is directly at the base of the route. Without touching the tree, the first 10 feet is awkward and technical, whereas grabbing the tree for balance, or pressing off of it with your tush, makes it an easy 5.8. The remainder of the climb is solid, and a great introductory slab climb.

7.   **Unknown 5.7** Unfortunately, this lieback flake is usually covered in a layer of soft green moss. Otherwise, it would be a whole-lotta fun. This route can be toproped from the two-bolt anchor on the right, or led traditionally.

SKYLINE BOULDER

Before you reach the slabs, you will pass by a 25-foot-tall boulder that rests at the top of the gully, below the house on the ridge. Although only three problems have been claimed, cleared, and named on the boulder, many more potential problems exist. Since the boulder has not seen much activity, watch out for loose holds, especially on the top.

1.   **Skyline Boulder Traverse V2** This 30-foot traverse begins on the south side of the rock and heads uphill and around the corner to the southeast. Nice long warm-up.

2.   **Summit or Plummet V5 R** If you enjoy overhanging pockets and slopers with long reaches and lots of air under your feet, you will love this problem. It leads from the ground up and over the northwest roof. Scary! Chris Summit, 2001.

3.   **Western Traverse V0+** Follow the western side of the boulder from the right to left edge, fifteen feet long. Can be continued into *Summit or Plummet*, making the problem a V6.

Geologist Larry Guenther worms his way up Bandito, The Grotto

East of the Bay Areas

THE GROTTO

Tucked away behind New Melones Lake in Jamestown this crag is unique and beautiful. Located on Table Mountain, the area has experienced development recently, with the majority of the routes put up within the past decade.

The columnar basalt provides a multitude of stellar cracks, as well as a fine selection of quality face climbs reaching up to 90 feet. Beautiful squared-off pillars form the base of the Main Wall of The Grotto. Above these pillars, the basalt is chunky and overhanging, never short of holds. Opposite the columns, shorter routes exist on The Ort Wall, while even shorter, more overhanging routes, lie on The Cave Wall.

This section highlights the more popular climbs located at and near the main area, otherwise known as The Pit. More than twenty-five traditional and sport routes exist here, ranging from 5.8 to 5.12d. The Welcome Wall, which has six routes, is also included. It is the first wall you come to on the main trail.

Four areas located close by at Table Mountain are not covered in this guide: Mid Wall, The Fissures, Gold Wall, and The Far Side. Mid Wall has less than ten routes, all 5.11s and 5.12s. The Fissures has at least twelve bolted sport routes. Two traditional lead climbs are 5.8 and under, but these are rated very poorly due to bad rock quality. Other than one 5.10d, routes are all 5.11s and 5.12s.

The Fissures is a popular area during the winter because the area receives sun much of the day. Several new bolted routes exist at The Gold Wall and a handful of routes are located at The Far Side. For a complete listing of routes for the Table Mountain area, see *A Guide to Table Mountain and Tuolumne Pass* by Grant Hiskes.

Area Geology: All of the rock at The Grotto and Table Mountain areas is columnar basalt, much like the basalt of the famous Devil's Tower in Wyoming. Often climbers and even geologists incorrectly assume the rock is two different types due to the structural differences between the large squared-off pillars at the base and the chunky, block-like overhanging upper rock.

Volcanic lava formed this rock 10 to 20 million years ago. The lava spread along the ground and started to cool. It started to solidify and jell; and when it cooled, it actually started to shrink, making cracks in the newborn rock. Near the top of the lava flow, the rock cooled much faster, forming cracks more rapidly, thus making blocks and jugs with flat angular surfaces (or sometimes resembling teardrops) that fit together. Below, where the rock took much longer to cool, the cracks formed very slowly and lined up perpendicular to the top of the flow. This is how the nice columns with the fairly uniform cracks were developed. You will need a good deal of the same-sized gear for traditionally leading many of the cracks from the ground on up.

Chris Summit

Richie Esquibel on Sidewinder, *Upper Main Wall of The Grotto, with The Fissures on the left and Gold Wall on the far left*

TRIP INFORMATION

Climbing Season: The best time to climb here is in the spring and fall. Summers in the Central Valley can be brutal, with temperatures soaring over 100 degrees. The Pit is much cooler than the other areas because it is usually shaded and 30 feet below ground level. Diehards can climb in the summer months but should plan on an early morning or late afternoon trip. Chalk up!

The Fissures offer warmer climbing during the wintertime and much drier rock than The Pit. Fog envelops the Central Valley during much of the winter, often causing damp conditions. Keep in mind that during the winter there is more moss in The Pit, increasing the "whoa!" factor on some of the climbs.

Fees: There are no fees at The Grotto. The crag is on BLM land. Shut the gates on the dirt road after entering and exiting to ensure good relations and easy access in the future.

Camping: Since The Grotto is located on BLM land, camping is legal. When looking for a spot to pitch a tent, watch out for cowpies. A nice flat area directly off the dirt road is located about 0.5 mile past the trail that leads up to The Pit and Welcome Wall. BLM rangers do frequent checks of the area. Pick up your garbage and completely extinguish any campfires.

If you want to stay at a bonafide campground, the closest is Lake Tulloch RV Campground and Marina. The address is 14448 Tulloch Dam Road. There are 125 spaces available, ranging from $17 to $28 each per night. You can reach the campground by calling (209) 881–0107; or better yet, (800) 894–CAMP. For on-line information, go to www.laketullochcampground.com.

Dogs: There are no restrictions on dogs. If you want to get your pooch down in The Pit, approach around the opposite side of the main trail and Welcome Wall (northwest). Walk around The Pit across a boulder field and reach a low angle approach feeding you in between Main Wall and Cave Wall.

Emergency Services: There are no call boxes for emergencies on or close to Shell Road, or Rawhide Road. Your best bet is a drive to the nearest gas station, Tesoro, at the corner of Rawhide Road and California 108.

There are two hospitals in Sonora, located 3 miles east of Rawhide Road on CA 108. The closest to the crag is Sonora Community Hospital, located on South Forest Road off California 49 entering Sonora. A larger hospital is Tuolumne General Hospital located at 101 Hospital Road in Sonora. The phone number is (209) 533-7100.

Water Sources: The nearest water sources are in Jamestown, less than 4 miles from the crag.

Telephones: Jamestown is also the closest place with a pay phone. There are numerous phones at gas stations and mini-marts along CA 108. A pay phone is located at the rear of the parking lot next to the Tesoro gas station.

Restrooms: The nearest restroom facilities are at gas stations on CA 108 in Jamestown.

Coffee Shops: There are two coffee shops very close to one another in Jamestown. Jamestown Coffee Emporium is located at 18202 Main Street, and Jamestown Café & Coffee House is located at 18141 Main Street. Main Street runs parallel to CA 108. Traveling east on CA 108, turn right on the street past Rawhide Road to get to Main Street.

There is also a little coffee shack called Day O! next to the Tesoro gas station at CA 108 and Rawhide Road. Day O! has decent brewed coffee and a wide variety of frou frou coffee drinks. The Day O! baristas are a very friendly bunch.

If you can't wait to get to Jamestown for coffee, a great source is in the city of Escalon. Yosemite Coffee Company is located on the west side of Escalon on California 120, behind Taco Bell.

Markets: The closest market is in Sonora. Save Mart is on the left side of CA 49 as you drive east into Sonora, 3 miles east of Rawhide Road. You will also pass markets along CA 120 in Escalon and Oakdale before you hop on CA 108 heading for Jamestown.

Brewpubs: Snowshoe Brewery is located in the town of Standard, only 7 miles from Jamestown. Several brews are available as well as great food. From CA 108 at Rawhide Road, drive east on CA 108 for 6.3 miles (passing the exit to Sonora) and turn right on Standard Road. Drive for 0.5 mile on Standard, and you will see the Snowshoe Brewery on the right side of the road.

Gas Stations: There are several gas stations along CA 108 in Jamestown. The closest to the crag is Tesoro at the corner of Rawhide Road and CA 108. Chevron, on the south side of CA 108 (0.5 mile west of Rawhide Road), has nice clean restrooms inside.

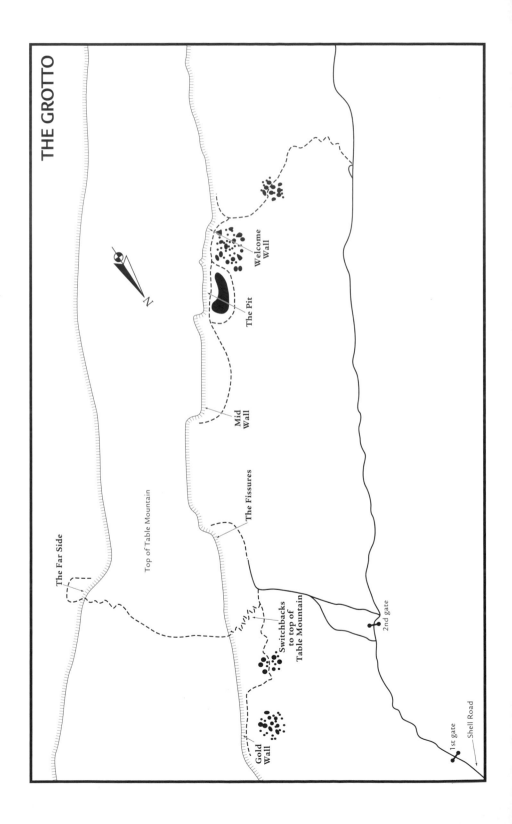

THE GROTTO

N

The Far Side

Top of Table Mountain

The Fissures

Mid Wall

The Pit

Welcome Wall

Switchbacks to top of Table Mountain

Gold Wall

2nd gate

1st gate

Shell Road

Directions: The distance between San Francisco and The Grotto is roughly 130 miles. From Interstate 80, head east over the Bay Bridge into the East Bay. Take Interstate 580 (eastbound) through Oakland and past Livermore, heading over Altamont Pass. Upon descending the pass, take Interstate 205 through Tracy, then merge onto CA 120 (eastbound), passing through Manteca and Oakdale. From Oakdale on CA 120, the distance to CA 108 is 43 miles. When traveling east on CA 120, the highway forks and CA 120 heads right (toward Yosemite) or continues straight, turning into CA 108 (eastbound). From this intersection, go 5.7 miles on CA 108 to Rawhide Road in Jamestown. Turn left on Rawhide Road and continue for 1.9 miles before turning left on Shell Road. Drive on Shell Road for 1.5 miles to where the road turns to dirt. A high-clearance vehicle can be helpful especially during wet months.

From the intersection of Shell Road and Rawhide Road, the distance on Shell to the first gate is 1.5 miles. To get to The Fissures and Gold Wall, drive 0.8 mile past the first gate and park just past the second gate. To get to The Pit and Welcome Wall, the distance from the first gate you pass through on Shell Road (this is also where the road turns to dirt) to the trailhead is 1.2 miles. You will pass a total of three fences on the dirt road, the first two with gates.

Approach: The walk from the dirt road to the crag should take less than twenty minutes. The foot trail is fairly apparent from the road. Opposite the lake, an upward sloping parking space and trail leads from the road up a narrow footpath to the right and through a wooded area. You will know you are on the right trail when you see a telephone pole directly on the trail only 25 yards from the road. The pole has the number "41" spray-painted on the base. Continue up the trail crossing over the bases of two trees and heading into a field of small mossy rocks. Hike up and across the rocks to continue on the dirt trail. Walk another 100 yards or so until you reach another larger field of rocks. Welcome Wall will be on your right-hand side. (Note: Watch out for poison oak!)

WELCOME WALL

This is the first wall (aptly named) you will see when hiking up the trail to the crag. There are six climbs on it ranging from 5.10a to 5.11c. Routes top out at 60 feet. Beware of bat guano, bird droppings, and rat pellets. All three may be on many key holds on *Swallow This* and *Wing of Bat*. This nuisance definitely downgrades the quality of these climbs.

1.   **Welcome Mat 5.10b** ★★ Seven bolts to a two-bolt anchor with a chain link on each. This 75-foot route is not well-traveled.

2.   **Keebler's Revenge 5.11a** ★★★ Six bolts to two-bolt anchor. Pumpy, technical, and sustained. Craig McClenahan, Phil Bone, and Danny Keebler, 1991.

3.   **Swallow This 5.11c** ★★ Five bolts to two-bolt chain anchor. Very difficult cruxy moves from the ground up past the second bolt. Many believe the grade should be changed to 5.11d. Craig McClenahan, 1991.

Welcome Wall, The Grotto

4. **Wing of Bat 5.10a ★★★** Five bolts to a two-bolt anchor shared with *Swallow This.* Watch out for bats hanging out in the undercling flake past the third bolt. Oodles of bird and bat poop on all of the critical holds.

5. **Uncle Remus 5.11a ★★★★** Nine bolts to two-bolt chain anchor. Good holds and bomber feet on overhanging basalt. This 85-foot route offers up some good fun! Danny Keebler, 1992.

5a. **Uncle Remus Direct Start 5.11a R ★★★★** Seven bolts to two-bolt chain anchor. This was originally the intended line for *Uncle Remus,* but the runout at the beginning kept many off the route. Later a different route setter added two bolts to the left creating the popular line. Danny Keebler, 1992.

6. **Roe vs. Wade 5.9 ★★** Six bolts to chains. Relaxed warm-up. A little chossy near the top. Belayer beware. Phil Bone, 1997.

THE PIT

The lower half of this area stays much cooler than the others because it is 30 to 40 feet below the ground level of Welcome and Mid Wall. One side of The Pit has short chunky climbs on it that top out at 30 feet, while the opposite wall has pillars and cracks that sail up to a second pitch of rock.

Lower Main Wall

Note that some cracks are neither named nor mentioned in this guide, including certain crack stemming possibilities. *A-C Devil Dog* is a good marker for finding routes here. It is the six-bolt climb on the most prominent column, which is about the width of a refrigerator.

1. **Prime Directive 5.10c R ★** Pro to 3″ for lower half, then seven bolts to two bolt chain anchor. The crack at the base is easy 5.8 climbing. An array of holds are available on overhanging rock that eases in difficulty after the fifth bolt. David Clay, 1995.

2. **Crack 5.9 ★★★★** Pro to 3″. Lots of hand and fist jamming. Solid pro

3. **Hole in the Wall 5.10a ★★** Pro to 2.5″. This crack has some loose plates midway up inside the crack. Plug in the gear.

4. **Three Fingered Jack 5.10b ★★★★** Pro to 3″. Fine hand and finger crack. Another great crack that loves eating up nuts and cams. Watch out for a little loose stuff at the top. Chains above for toproping or lowering. Grant Hiskes, 1990s.

5. **Snake Bite 5.11b ★★★** Pro to 2.5″. Easy climbing up and over a bomber roof, then good balance and a love for tweaked fingers is needed for the crux. Chains above for anchor. Peter Croft, 1989.

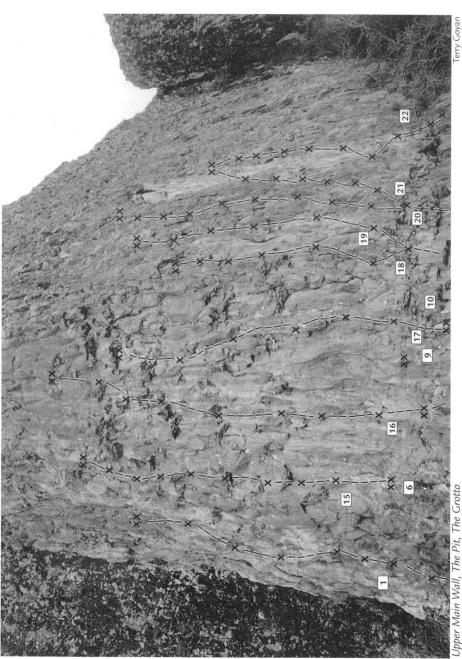

Terry Goyan

Upper Main Wall, The Pit, The Grotto

Terry Goyan

Lower Main Wall, The Pit, The Grotto

6. **Rawhide 5.10d ★★★★★** Pro to 2.5". Beautiful finger to hand crack. Two cold shuts anchor it. Also can be set up as a toprope. Grant Hiskes, 1990s.

7. **Mens Crisis Center 5.11d ★★** Pro to 2" with four bolts available on second half of route. Phil Bone, 1990.

8. **Table Manners 5.8 ★★★** Pro to 3". Use both cracks and stem away. Using only one crack increases the difficulty.

9. **A-C Devil Dog 5.10c ★★★★★** Six bolts to two-bolt anchor. Funky smear and slap moves up a very tall refrigerator masquerading as a rock. Anchors to the left and right of it. Mike Stewart, 1991.

10. **Bandito 5.8 ★★★** Pro to 4". There is a two-bolt chain anchor on top. Good crack for learning how to place pro. Goes from hands to fist jams with an abundance of rests in between.

11. **To Pin or Not to Be 5.11a ★★★★** Thin pro with five bolts on face. The pin is gone, but of course, the crack remains. There is a two-bolt anchor above. Delicate climbing on two thin cracks. Craig McClenahan, 1991.

12. **Moss Critique 5.11b ★★** Thin pro. Slippery and mossy. Challenging crack to a two-bolt anchor. Phil Bone and Craig McClenahan, 1991.

13. **Trigger Finger 5.10a ★** Pro to 2.5". Dirty and a little mossy.

14. **Go with the Flow 5.9 ★★★★★** Pro to 2.5". Quality finger to hand crack.

Upper Main Wall

This section of wall contains some of the best face climbs at The Grotto. All of the lines here are 5.11c or harder, with the exception of one 5.10b and a 5.10c.

15. **Ejection Seat 5.11d ★★★★** Eight bolts to two-bolt anchor. Overhanging and sustained. Bomber hidden holds exist; you just need to have the strength to hang out and find them. John Williams, 1993–1994.

16. **Bombardier (a.k.a. Accessive Force) 5.12d/13a ★★★★** Seven bolts to two-bolt anchor. Although this climb has been called *Accessive Force* for years, the actual given name is *Bombardier*, which is the crew member who releases the bombs from a military aircraft. Who needs the seventh bolt anyway? (A little hard to clip.) Bombs away! Tom Addison, 1993–1994.

17. **Flight Simulator 5.12b ★★★★★** Five bolts to two-bolt anchor. What could be better than a burn with some long sequential moves right when you feel you are going to peel? Takes flight directly above *A-C Devil Dog*. Craig McClenahan, 1993–1994.

18. **Premature Ejection 5.12c ★★** Six bolts to two-bolt anchor. Cruxy moves past the third bolt heading over a roof. Troy Corliss, 1995.

19. **Journey to Find the Sun 5.12a ★★★** Six bolts to two-bolt anchor. Tackle first crux in the first 10 feet, then get ready for stiff technical moves after fifth bolt. Craig McClenahan, 1993–1994.

20. **Squeeler 5.11c/d ★★★★** Nine bolts to two-bolt anchor. Bomber holds on a severe overhang. The longest and highest route on the Upper Main Wall of The Pit. Grant Hiskes and Ken Yeager, 1995.

21. **Sidewinder 5.11d ★★★** Seven bolts to two-bolt anchor. Heads up over Go with the Flow, then winds to the right to share anchors with *Chicken Ranch Bingo*. Difficult crux between fifth and sixth bolt. Dave Bangston, 1995.

22. **Chicken Ranch Bingo 5.10b ★★★★★** Nine bolts to two-bolt anchor. Long overhanging route with huge chunky holds and great rests. Long draws or slings recommended for first and fourth bolts. Grant Hiskes, 1993.

Mishon Martin warming up on Sidesaddle, *Ort Wall*

ORT WALL

The Ort Wall (an abbreviation for Short Wall) has six bolted face climbs reaching up to 35 feet in length. This wall is on the opposite side of The Pit from the Main Wall. See photo on page 182.

1. **Misperception 5.10c ★** Three bolts to chain anchor. Easy start to slopey crux before the third bolt.

2. **Ort Man Complex 5.10c ★★** Four bolts to chain anchor shared with Misperception. Crux between third and fourth bolts. Phil Bone, 2000.

3. **Clip, Clip, Wow 5.10d ★★★★** Five bolts to cold shuts. Pumpy and over-hanging.

4. **Geronimo 5.11b ★★★** Six bolts to cold shuts. Short and stout climbing on overhanging jugs with a few nasty slopers on the way. Grant Hiskes and Ken Yaeger, 1994.

5. **Color Coded Quickdraws 5.10b ★★★★** Four bolts to chains. Great warm-up on slightly overhanging jugs.

6. **Sidesaddle 5.9 ★★★★** Five bolts to cold shuts. Very popular warm-up. Crux near third bolt.

Ort Wall, The Grotto

Cave Wall, The Grotto

CAVE WALL

This is by far the shortest wall and the most overhanging wall at The Grotto. Routes range between 15 and 25 feet long. Power routes relying on bouldery moves live here—all 5.12s.

1. **Grotto Monkey 5.12a/b** ★★★★★ Four bolts to cold shuts. Juggy and reachy sustained route. Crux near base. Dave Bangston, 1990.

2. **Dwarf Toss 5.12a** ★★★★ Four bolts to cold shuts shared with *Grotto Monkey*. If you are tall enough, (about 6 feet) reach straight up to crimps just right of the first bolt and yank yourself up. If this is too high, start left of the first bolt and traverse a couple of feet to the right on overhanging slopes. Watch for the loose horn above the first bolt. Bouldery moves to third bolt, the climb then eases up past the fourth bolt and to the anchors. Pre-clip the first bolt. Phil Bone, 1990.

3. **Sasquatch 5.12b** ★★★★ Five bolts to cold shuts shared with *Grotto Monkey* and *Dwarf Toss*. Pre-clip the first bolt. Dave Bangston, 1990.

4. **High Intensity Discharge 5.12a** ★ Two bolts to two-bolt anchor. Danny Keebler, 1991.

CONSUMNES RIVER GORGE

Consumnes is not exactly a hop, skip, and jump away from the Bay Area, but it is a great crag for a few reasons: weather, abundance of climbs with good approaches, and a mix that will please beginners and veteran climbers alike. When the seasons have turned and the San Francisco Bay Area is on the chilly side, or just plain rainy, chances are pleasant weather is waiting for you in Placerville. Between Sacramento and Lake Tahoe, where Consumnes is located, the climate is often warmer in the early spring and late fall than in the Bay Area.

Other appetizing details may lure you to Consumnes. A wide array of cracks on choice granite is concentrated in a very small area, which means less hiking and more climbing. A four-pitch wall, directly across the river, has eight multip-itch climbs and several fine routes at the base.

There are at least 150 established routes at Consumnes, so climbers can be quite busy for some time. Consumnes is also a great place for beginners to practice toproping, setting pro, and crushing their toes inside cracks. Nearly every route at Consumnes can be toproped thanks to the numerous bolts located along the tops of cliffs and boulders. The walk-offs are a breeze.

Consumnes is divided into five areas: Buck's Bar Dome, Gutenberger Wall, Struggler Cliff, Ten Minute Cliff, Midway Rocks, and Granite Cove. Included in this section are twenty highlighted climbs, which are located in the most popular areas, Buck's Bar Dome and Gutenberger Wall.

For a complete guide to this extensive crag, pick up a copy of *Rock Climbs of*

Lynn Cuthbertson finding the right piece on Dinkum

Consumnes River Gorge written by William H. Cottrell and published by El Dorado Publishing. It is available at Shoreline Mountain Products, San Rafael, California; (415) 455–1000.

Area Geology: Everyone loves granite, and coarsely grained granite is what you will get at Consumnes. Some climbs are covered with large friendly knobs and chunks, while other sections of granite, washed over the years by river water, are slick as ice. This area has the same type of granite as the rock located in most of the Lake Tahoe region. It mainly consists of quartz and orthoclase feldspar.

About 175 million years ago, the continental crust moved upward. When the crust cooled, while still below the surface, granite was formed and later exposed due to erosion. If the crust did not cool before reaching the surface, eruptions would have occurred, thus making volcanoes such as those in the Cascades.

TRIP INFORMATION

Climbing Season: Consumnes is a fine cold weather crag. When most of Northern California is iced over (or too soggy), Placerville is often cool and temperate. Weather does not come in as rapidly as in the mountainous regions further east. Summers here can be very hot, but certain features such as the Great Chimney at Buck's Bar Dome offer refreshment with nice cool temperatures inside. Climbers can also find quite a few shady, cooler areas on the east side of the river in the height of summer.

Be warned! Temperatures on the multi-pitch Gutenberger Wall (facing southwest) can often soar well over 100 degrees, making climbing here in the summer grueling to endure. The heat draws climbers and hikers alike into the frigid Consumnes River where carved granite watering holes offer relief. Bear in mind, after a significant rain or in the early spring, the river is often too wild for swimming (not to mention, it's freezing cold).

Fees: There are no fees at Consumnes. Take care not to leave any valuables in your vehicle here!

Camping: Most of the land in and around Placerville is privately owned and public camping is limited. A KOA campground in Shingle Springs, 6 miles west of Placerville, has 112 sites. The sites are pricey ($22-$25), so take advantage of the showers and swimming pool. From Placerville, take U.S. Highway 50 (westbound) for 5 miles and exit at Shingle Springs Drive. Turn left (west) on Rock Barn Road, which leads directly to the KOA campground. The address is 4655 Rock Barn Road, Shingle Springs. Call (800) 562–4197 or (530) 676–CAMP for information on availability.

Dogs: There are no restrictions on dogs at Consumnes River Gorge. It is a good idea to keep them on the north side of the river, where Buck's Bar is located.

Emergency Services: Marshall Hospital in Placerville is the closest emergency care facility to the crag. Heading back toward Placerville, it is located on Marshall Street off Cedar Ravine Road. Signs direct you up Marshall to the hospital. It is roughly 8 miles from the crag.

Water Sources: There are no fountains or water sources at the crag. A water purifier or iodine tablets would be good to have on hand in case the river water is the only option. The closest drinking water is in Placerville.

Telephones: No pay phones exist near the crag. Once again, Placerville is the nearest option.

Restrooms: No restrooms exist at or near the climbing areas. There is a public restroom next door to the Placerville Courthouse on Main Street at Bedford Avenue, just a few blocks west of the intersection of Main Street and Cedar Ravine Road.

Coffee Shops: When driving through Placerville, don't pass up the chance to visit the Placerville Coffee House. The rear of the establishment is an old mine used in the days of the California Gold Rush. The dark, musty tunnels have a few lamps scattered about, as well as a chair here and there. Experience the interesting ambience over a cup of coffee. Sandwiches and a wide variety of smoothies are offered. Placerville Coffee House is located at the corner of Main Street and Cedar Ravine Road in Placerville.

Markets: An Albertson's is located on Main Street in Placerville. When driving eastbound on Main Street, go 3 blocks past (east of) Cedar Ravine Road and look for Albertson's on your right.

Brewpubs: Jack Russell Brewing Co. in the tiny town of Camino offers good beer and a nice environment. Located in the area known as Apple Hill, the brewery is modeled after an English farm brewery with wide open space and grassy fields surrounding it. The majority of the seating is at outdoor picnic tables with benches. An overweight pot-bellied pig can often be seen roaming the area searching for morsels.

The downside of Jack Russell Brewing Co. is its operating hours—cut short Sunday through Thursday, closing at 5:00 P.M. The brewery is open late Friday and Saturday, basically until the crowd dies down. A local East Indian restaurant trucks food into the brewery, but it is only served Friday evenings between 5:00 and 8:00 P.M.

To get to the brewery, drive back from the crag to U.S. 50 and head east. Drive 7.8 miles and turn left at the Camino exit, crossing the highway. Make your first right on Carson Road and drive less than 1 mile to Larsen Drive. Turn left on Larsen and follow the curvy road for 1.3 miles past barns and farm animals. The Jack Russell Brewing Co. is at 2380 Larsen Drive on the north side of the road.

Gas Stations: Several gas stations are located along Main Street in Placerville. There is a Shell at Main Street and Spring Street. Directly across, there is a Chevron.

Directions: From San Francisco, take Interstate 80 (eastbound) across the Bay Bridge and through the East Bay heading toward Sacramento (about 80 miles northeast). When you reach Sacramento, head east on U.S. 50 toward Lake Tahoe, traveling 39.4 miles to Placerville. Make a right turn off U.S. 50 onto Spring Street in Placerville. Immediately turn left on Main Street, drive 0.5 mile, and turn right on Cedar Ravine Road. Drive for 5.4 miles and turn left on Pleasants Valley Road, then go only 100 yards before turning right on Buck's Bar Road. Drive 2.9 miles and park on either side of the road. For the alternate approach (if there is no parking here), head downhill for an additional 0.5 mile and park next to the bridge that crosses over Consumnes River.

Approach: There are two paths to approach the crag. They start at the two main parking areas. From the upper (first) parking area, a good trail leads downhill and winds down to the top of Buck's Bar Dome. You can rappel down from the top, where there are several bolts; or if you continue to the right on the trail, it will lead you around and down to the base of the climbs at Buck's Bar Dome.

The lower parking area, next to the one-lane bridge, offers a trail that is above the river and follows it downstream, also arriving atop Buck's Bar Dome. This

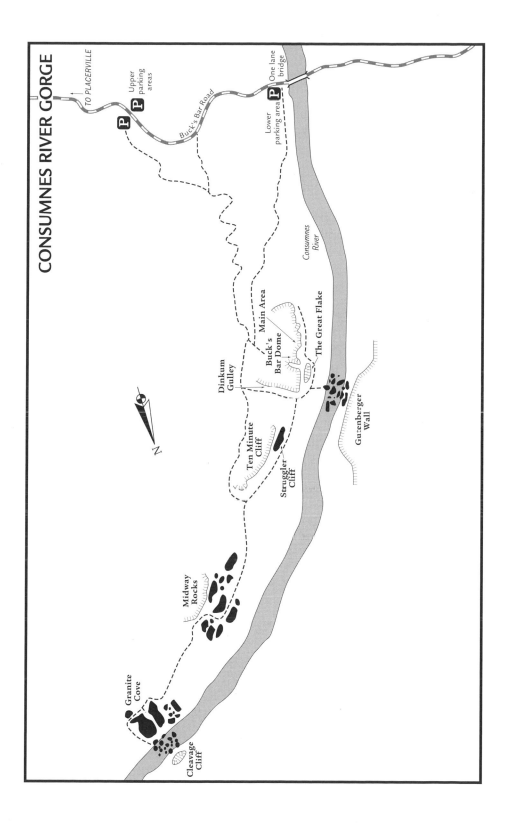

CONSUMNES RIVER GORGE

TO PLACERVILLE

Upper parking areas

Buck's Bar Road

One lane bridge

Lower parking area

Consumnes River

N

Main Area

Dinkum Gulley

Buck's Bar Dome

The Great Flake

Gutenberger Wall

Ten Minute Cliff

Struggler Cliff

Midway Rocks

Granite Cove

Cleavage Cliff

trail is a little harder to read. Make sure to follow the widest branch that leads slightly up and right. When you can see Gutenberger Wall on your left, you are close to Buck's Bar Dome. Look for bolts near the edge of a very large ledge.

Buck's Bar Dome

This is the most popular climbing area at Consumnes. It has the highest concentration of routes in a small spot. Topropes can be set up on virtually every climb due to the large number of bolts and trees. The routes here range from 15 to 30 feet in length. The following routes include some of the quality climbs at Buck's. The first route is located in Dinkum Gully. Routes two through six are on The Great Flake.

1. **Dinkum 5.9 ★★★★★** Pro to 2″. This fine finger to hand crack is located in the center of the wall at Dinkum Gulley. The route is not marked on the photo, but the gully is shown on the overview map for the area.

2. **Dan's Delight 5.9 ★★** Pro to 4″. Fist crack with crux off the deck. Located on the east side of The Great Flake.

3. **Training Pants 5.8 ★★** Pro to 5″. A little lieback action, along with good holds, in this wide crack make a fun, easy climb.

4. **Awful Width 5.8 ★★★** Pro to 5″. Not so awful because it's less than 20 feet.

5. **Mangler 5.9 ★★★** Pro to 5″. Begins pretty wide, then slims down for the finish.

6. **Live and Learn 5.8 ★★★** Pro to 3″. This climb, on the right side of The Great Flake, takes great pro and provides you with fine finger and hand locks.

The Great Flake, Buck's Bar Dome

Doug Wright "head jamming" on Unconquerable, *Buck's Bar Dome*

Main Area routes at Buck's Bar Dome

7. **Chamberlin's Chimney 5.8 ★★** Enter The Great Chimney and head back to the cool stone where you will need to squeeze your way to the top.

8. **Fingerprint 5.12b ★★** If you love climbing over minuscule holds and smearing your way up a nearly vertical route, this toprope line is for you.

9. **Unconquerable 5.8 ★★★★★** Pro to 5". A scary, yet conquerable, lead.

10. **Test Piece 5.8 ★★★★** Pro to 3". This route gets very greasy in the heat of summer. Crux midway up climb.

11. **Adhesion 5.10c ★★★** An abundance of slopers with a nice grain of granite help you to the anchors on this toprope line.

Gutenberger Wall

This is the only area on the east side of the river with the exception of Cleavage Cliff (across the river from Granite Cove), which lies farther downstream and currently has only two climbs on it.

Gutenberger has four-pitch routes on exposed slab. Most routes begin at the Grand Central Belay Station, which is the beginning of the second pitch. Three basic lines lead you to this station. These routes are numbered 4, 5, and 6. Be aware that many lines on the upper three slab pitches are runout with long, painfully bumpy falls possible. The top of the wall holds two separate anchors, reachable by all of the climbs. The eight multipitch routes take gear and may sport a few bolts where the cracks disappear. Some routes on Gutenberger Wall are listed here.

Gutenberger Wall, Consumnes River Gorge

Grand
Central
Belay

4

5

fp

Approach
Boulder

6

Routes on first pitch of Gutenberger Wall, Consumnes River Gorge

1. **Lichen Us 5.9 ★★** This newer route has a few more bolts than most of the other routes on this wall.

1a. **Lichen Us Variation 5.9 ★★**

2. **Gutenberger Wall Direct 5.7 ★★** Easy exposed climbing up a well-protected crack.

3. **Gutenberger Wall 5.8 R ★** From the Grand Central Belay Station at the second pitch, the route travels right and up the right side of the wall.

4. **Dihedral Direct 5.10d ★★★★** Pro to 3″. This climb begins directly above the river in a crack leading up a dihedral, then goes over a roof and into the crack of Gutenberger Wall Direct. From there it

Unknown Climber on Dihedral Direct, *Gutenberger Wall*

leads straight up the middle of the wall. Although short, this climb is challenging and appealing. A bolt (sent from angels) is in reach just before pulling over the roof.

5. **Dihedral Bypass 5.9 ★★** Start heading up the dihedral and then move right and up to easier climbing.

6. **The Easy Way Up 5.7 ★** Obviously a popular route up to Grand Central Belay Station. Begin on the Approach Boulder (directly below Grand Central Belay Station) in the river. Head up and over the right corner onto the wall, continuing to the right. Traverse right to a corner, then change direction, heading left and up past a bolt and a shaky flake to Grand Central.

Struggler Cliff

This cliff is just a few moments downstream from Buck's Bar Dome. It offers six toproping face routes ranging from 5.5 to 5.10d. Two off-width cracks are available, a 5.8 and a 5.9. Finally, a 5.8 lieback crack is just left of the center of the cliff. See photo on page 194.

Ten Minute Cliff

This cliff lies directly behind and downstream from Struggler Cliff. The area is frequented due to a high quality 5.12 finger crack named Ten Minute Crack. Seven other climbs, rated 5.8 through 5.10, share the 25-foot cliff. Two of the seven are quality routes. See photo on page 194.

Struggler Cliff, Consumnes River Gorge

Ten Minute Cliff, Consumnes River Gorge

1. **Ten Minute Crack 5.12 ★★★★★** Small pro. Bomber finger locks and jams.

2. **Scorpio 5.8 ★★★★** Takes small pro. This thin crack leads rightward and diagonally on the right side of the wall.

3. **Mastophilia 5.10 ★★★** This toprope line begins underneath the first half of Scorpio and moves straight up over Scorpio on knobs to the top.

Midway Rocks

This cliff is another five minutes farther downstream from Struggler Cliff and Ten Minute Cliff. Several large boulders are clumped in a small area with holds few and far between. Most of the face climbs here are 5.11s or 5.12s, and the five available cracks are 5.10–5.12.

Granite Cove

This very small area is the furthest downstream at Consumnes. There are two good 5.11 cracks on rock reaching almost 30 feet and a small handful of toproping face climbs. Across the river is Cleavage Cliff, which only has two routes on it—chimneys going at 5.7 and 5.9.

VACAVILLE BOULDERS

Who would have thought Vacaville, once known for the Nut Tree (a restaurant and some gift shops) and an abundance of cows, offered great bouldering in an attractive setting? Most Bay Area residents have driven right by this fine area on the way to the Sierra or other locales, unaware of the bouldering potential that awaits.

Located less than 2 miles from Interstate 80, the boulders lie scattered about the rolling hills of the Vacaville Open Space. You will share these hills with herds of cattle, so watch your step. Surrounding the hills, there are scores of large, new, nearly identical-looking homes—many have big blue pools in the back yards.

Vacaville translates in Spanish to "cow town." Recently Vacaville has become a fast-growing suburb. Climbers have found humor in this homogenized bedroom community, giving boulder problems such names as "Cow Tipping," "Suburban Hell Hole," and "Barf."

Vacaville may lack the diversity and culture found closer to San Francisco, but Vacavillians do not struggle with exorbitant rents and limited parking spaces. Besides, all that really matters is that Vacaville has its quantity and quality of pillow basalt in check and ready for fun!

Area Geology: These boulders are the same rock type as the boulders at Putah Creek. They have been described as pillow basalt in other guides. Geologists now know that they are actually columnar basalt, a rock type 80 to 90 million years younger than pillow basalt. For a complete geological description read the area geology on Putah Creek Boulders.

TRIP INFORMATION

Climbing Season: Located 45 miles east of San Francisco, away from coastal breezes and fog, Vacaville gets hot in the summertime. Between June and August, chances are likely that you will need lots of chalk and brushes for greasy holds if you are bent on pinching the dark gray basalt.

Fees: There are no fees for treading on the land of Vacaville Open Space.

Camping: Although it is deemed "open space," it is not open enough for camping. The closest legal campsite is at Lake Solano Campground in Winters, 19 miles away. This campground is located on the south side of Putah Creek off Pleasants Valley Road. After dusk, the gates are closed and camp arrivals are not permitted. Campsites are $8.00 during the off-season (October through March) and $15 during the busy season (April through September). There are ninety sites available, sixty on a first-come, first-serve basis. The campground requires all dogs staying there to have a rabies vaccination certificate. Reservations can be made by calling (530) 795–2990, seven days a week between the hours of 9:00 A.M. and 2:00 P.M.

Dogs: There are no regulations regarding dogs at the Vacaville Boulders, but Lake Solano Campground requires all dogs to have a current rabies vaccination certificate.

Emergency Services: The nearest hospital is Vaca Valley Hospital, located 2 miles from the boulders at 1000 Nut Tree Road.

To get there, head back toward I-80 on Browns Valley Parkway. Turn right onto Allison Drive and cross over the freeway. Go 2 blocks and turn left on Ulatis Drive. The hospital is located at the intersection of Ulatis Drive and Nut Tree Road.

Water Sources: Unless you like drinking from an old bathtub generally used only by cows, you will need to drive back toward I-80 on Browns Valley Parkway to find water at Centennial Park, which is located south of Browns Valley Drive.

Telephones: Centennial Park on Browns Valley Parkway has a pay phone.

Restrooms: Clean restrooms are located at Centennial Park on Browns Valley Parkway. The park is open until dusk every day of the week.

Coffee Shops: Few options exist on the north side of the freeway where the boulders are located. For better tasting coffee, head back over I-80 on Allison Drive. Go 2 blocks and turn left on Elmira Road. Continue on Elmira until you pass Nut Tree Road where you will find Bay Coffee Co. in a shopping center on your left.

Markets: Ralph's Grocery Store is located at the corner of Elmira Road and Nut Tree Road on the south side of I-80.

Brewpubs: There are no brewpubs in Vacaville. If you like stale beer and nachos (just like the ones at the monster truck shows), you can stop by City Sports Bar & Grill at 155 Browns Valley Parkway. Video games and a bowling alley are also provided for hours of fine entertainment.

Chain restaurants like Chevy's, Fresh Choice, and Applebee's Bar & Grill are on the south side of the freeway near all of the factory outlets. Otherwise, you are better off heading to Davis (farther east) or returning to the Bay Area for better fare.

Gas Stations: A Shell is located on the north side of I-80 near Allison Drive.

Directions: From San Francisco, head east over the Bay Bridge and follow the Eastshore Freeway (I-80) east past Vallejo and Fairfield. In Vacaville, exit at the Allison Drive/Nut Tree Parkway and head left over the freeway—north on Allison. Turn left onto Browns Valley Parkway. You are now entering suburbia . . . turn left on Wrentham Drive. There are two main outcroppings.

To get to Woodcrest Boulders from Wrentham Drive, turn left on Woodcrest Drive and park almost immediately. Pass a yellow gate marked Vacaville Open Space and walk up a gravel road leading to a trail on your right near a water trough/bathtub. You will need to hop a short fence to follow the trail up to the boulders.

To find Hillcrest Boulders, continue driving on Wrentham Drive and turn right onto Vaca Valley Parkway. Drive a few more short blocks and turn left on Hillcrest Drive. Hillcrest is straight for a couple of hundred feet and then makes a sharp left after about 75 yards. Park here at the turn. A gate to the open space will be in front of you. A prominent trail leads past a large boulder (Scott's Rock) and up a hillside.

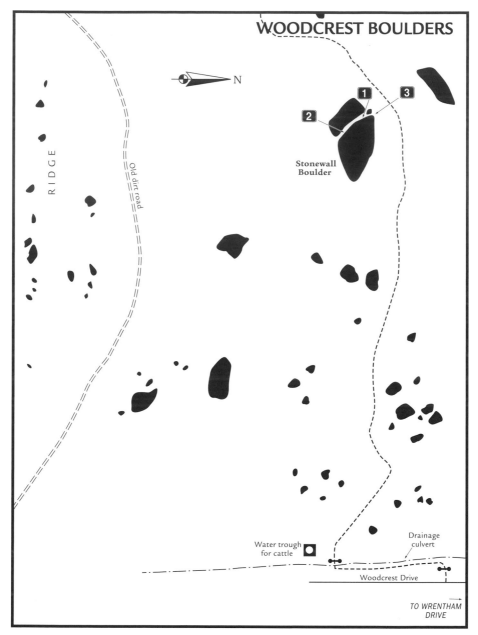

WOODCREST BOULDERS

Most climbers would agree that the finer bouldering problems are located here. You will find several V0 through V3s, as well as three V5s and a V7. This is a great place to fine tune your sit-starts because there are a whole lot of them. The extremely grippy sandpaper-like holds on certain rocks make it seem "like the first time."

The manmade stone wall surrounding the largest boulder is a great place to meet up with friends. It is easily recognized due to its large size and stone wall. It has a great view. There are three notable bouldering problems here.

Heads up for potentially hazardous loose rock on some of the boulders.

Ross MacKenzie on Stonewall Arête, Woodcrest Boulders

1.   **Nutcracker V2** This problem begins inside the dark, cave-like area between the Stonewall Boulder and its little brother leaning next to it. The problem starts right and goes up and left following a crack.

2.   **Buttcracker V5** This problem has a fitting name because, if you fail, your arse will not be the same for quite some time. Begin sitting near the left side of the wall inside the cave. Head straight up on poor holds.

3.   **Stonewall Arête V2/V3** Reachy moves straight up and over the top.

HILLCREST BOULDERS

These boulders do not see nearly as much activity as Woodcrest Boulders, but there are quite a few good problems here. Scott's Rock was named after Berkeley resident Scott Frye. He was the first to complete the V8/V9 traverse, which usually starts on the left and moves to the right around the rock.

In addition to Scott's Rock, you will pass several more boulders if you follow the trails uphill. At least four of these boulders have established problems. Most of these problems go at V1 to V3, and there are a few highball problems where a crash pad comes in handy. For detailed bouldering problems and more information on the Vacaville Boulders, see *The Wine Country Rocks* by Chris Summit, which is available at Shoreline Mountain Products and Bay Area climbing gyms.

See the map for Hillcrest Boulders on page 200.

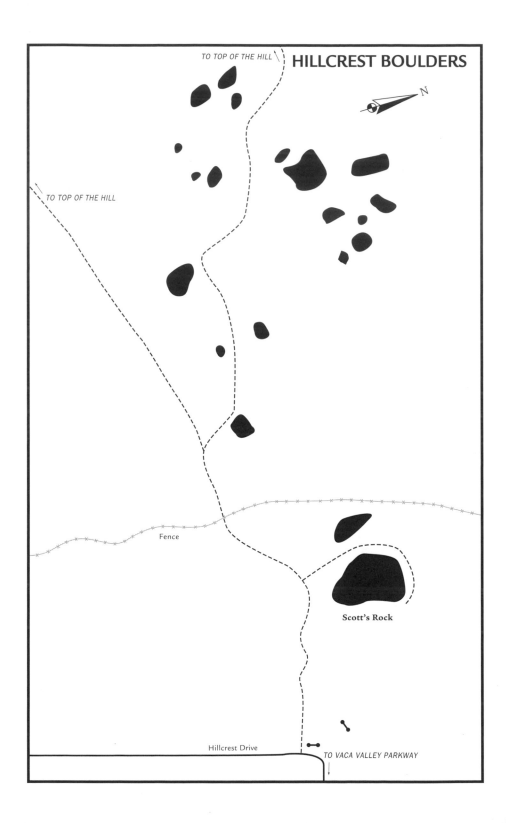

HILLCREST BOULDERS

N

TO TOP OF THE HILL

Fence

Scott's Rock

Hillcrest Drive

TO VACA VALLEY PARKWAY

PUTAH CREEK BOULDERS

Putah Creek is a great destination for climbers who live east of San Francisco. Five main boulders have developed problems ranging from V0 to V8, with more difficult problems possible. The boulders lie on the edge of Putah Creek, which offers an inviting way to cool off after a heated bouldering session, especially when temperatures in the town of Winters often soar over 100 degrees in the summertime.

There are five main boulders, all shown on the overview drawing. In addition, there are four smaller boulders to the east, two of which sport some nice V0s. Putah Creek landings are generally good on flat dirt or grass. A crash pad may be helpful for some of the highball problems that reach up to 15 feet. Be aware that poison oak is present in large quantities!

Area Geology: The boulders at Putah Creek and Vacaville are made of columnar basalt. They have previously been described by many geologists and climbers as pillow basalts, but current specialists in the geology field now believe they are indeed columnar basalts. When comparing columnar basalt and pillow basalt, the differences are great. Columnar basalt is blocky with flat surfaces that fit together, whereas pillow basalt is smooth, rounded, and blobby, appearing much like oranges stacked together. Columnar basalt was formed from on-land volcanic activity 10-20 million years ago, whereas pillow basalt was formed underneath the ocean more than 100 million years ago.

When the lava flowed from the volcano, it started to cool on the ground. As it cooled, it thickened and became jello-like. It shrank a little as it was cooling and formed cracks. This is the same process that makes mud cracks (seen in mudflats), or puddles that are drying up from sun and evaporation.

This rock is part of the Lovejoy Basalt, meaning it was basalt flows from the Sierra Nevada Range that moved to the coast of California. These coastal ranges were later lifted up and the boulders rolled down hills resting between the California Coast and the Sierra.

TRIP INFORMATION

Climbing Season: Since the town of Winters is inland, east of San Francisco and the coastal ranges, the climate is dry and usually warmer than areas along the San Francisco Bay. This makes Putah a good wintertime crag. The rock is also dense, so it dries quickly. In the heat of the summer, most of the rock is very greasy. It is wise to plan on bouldering in the early morning or late afternoon when the rock is cooler.

Fees: There are no fees for parking or enjoying the Putah Creek Boulders.

Camping: Lake Solano Campground is only 4 miles east of the boulders. It is located on the south side of Putah Creek off of Pleasants Valley Road. No camp arrivals are permitted after dusk.

Campsites are $8.00 during the off-season (October through March) and $15.00 during the busy season (April through September). There are ninety sites

Bill Granados on Heavy Metal Traverse, *Putah Creek Boulders*

available, sixty on a first-come, first-serve basis. Reservations are made by calling (530) 795–2990, seven days a week between the hours of 9:00 A.M. and 2:00 P.M.

Dogs: There are no restrictions for dogs at the boulders, but a rabies vaccination certificate is required if camping with a pooch at Lake Solano Campground.

Emergency Services: The closest hospital is in Davis, 11 miles away. Sutter Davis Hospital is at 2000 Sutter Place. The phone number is (530) 756–6440.

To get there, head back (northeast) on California 128. Cross over Interstate 505 and continue east. This becomes West Covell Boulevard. The hospital is on your left at the corner of Sutter Place. If you drive to California 113, you have gone too far.

Water Sources: Pardesha Gas Station, at the corner of CA 128 and Pleasants Valley Road, is the nearest source of water. Solano County Park, on the south side of Putah Creek along Pleasants Valley Road, also has water suitable for drinking.

Telephones: Pardesha Gas Station, 4 miles east of the boulders on CA 128, has a pay phone. The campground also has a pay phone. For emergencies, there are call boxes along CA 128.

Restrooms: The Solano County Regional Park has the closest public restroom to the boulders. CA 128 near Interstate 505 offers several possibilities, including a Chevron near the freeway interchange.

Coffee Shops: Berryessa Sporting Goods & Mini Market has an espresso bar inside. This fisherman's pit stop is next to the Towne and Country Market on CA 128, less than a mile west of I-505.

Markets: If traveling west on CA 128 from I-505, you will pass Towne and Country Market.

Brewpubs: The closest actual brewery, Sudwerks, is in Davis, about 21 miles from the crag. The brewery, a favorite of students and faculty at the University of California at Davis, has great beer and a nice outdoor patio, but the food is hit and miss—greasy french fries, salads with soggy croutons, and burgers. From the boulders, drive eastbound on CA 128 past I-505. Continue on CA 128, where the road will become West Covell Boulevard. Turn right onto CA 113 heading southbound toward San Francisco and Sacramento. Exit on Russell Boulevard toward Davis and turn left. Drive east on Russell Boulevard for 1.3 miles. Bear left on Fifth Street and drive 0.5 mile. Turn right on L Street and finally turn left on Second Street. Look for Sudwerks at 2001 Second Street.

There are a number of smaller bars close to the boulders, but most of these do not offer food. Irish Pub & Coffeehouse is located in Winters at Railroad Avenue (CA 128) and Main Street.

Gas Stations: A Chevron is located on CA 128 at I-505. Closer to the crag is Pardesha Gas Station, 3 miles west of I-505, on CA 128.

Directions: From San Francisco, the quickest route to the Putah Creek Boulders is eastbound on Interstate 80 and north on I-505. Continue for 11 miles and exit

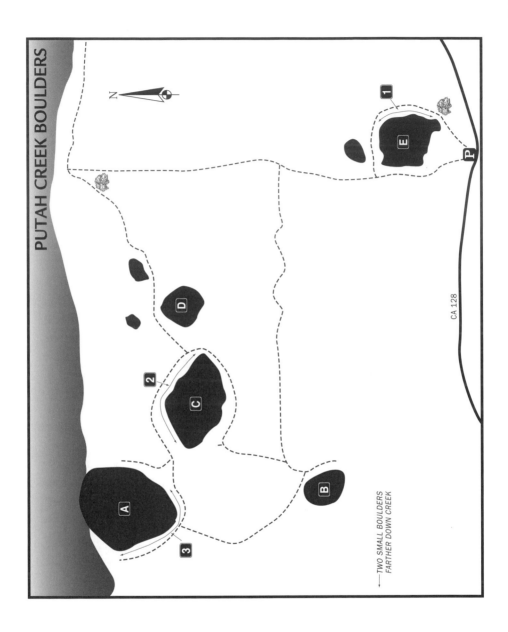

PUTAH CREEK BOULDERS

N

E
1
P
D
C
2
A
3
B

CA 128

TWO SMALL BOULDERS
FARTHER DOWN CREEK

at CA 128 (west) toward Lake Berryessa. Drive 7.5 miles to mile marker 2.32 on the right (north) side of the road. A dirt pullout is on the left side opposite the mile marker, and a boulder is visible just off the road.

PUTAH CREEK BOULDERS

1. **Roadside Traverse V7** This traverse is located on the "E" boulder next to the parking pullout. Long, difficult moves from the right moving uphill and left.

2. **Heavy Metal Traverse V4** This traverse is located on the "C" boulder. Start on the far right of the south side (creek side) of the boulder and traverse left around to the western side.

3. **Welcome to Whine Country V8** One of the more popular problems at Putah Creek, this traverse is located on the main boulder marked "A." Usually traversed from the left to the right.

Other Areas

GENOCIDE ROCK

This rock is in a beautiful location overlooking the Golden Gate Bridge and close to Fort Baker. The rock is nearly 30 feet high and has a wide variety of boulder problems and toproping possibilities. The northwestern side is very overhanging. Opposite the overhang is 5.2 climbing that can take you to the top. There are cracks and interesting squared-off edges on the north and east side.

Directions: The rock is located on the eastern hill above the intersection of Conzelman Road and McCullough Road. It is 50 yards above the Coastal Trailhead on a hill. Conzelman is the farthest southerly road, north of the Golden Gate Bridge.

From U.S. Highway 101 and Conzelman Road, head west on Conzelman Road until you come to the first road on your right, which is McCullough Road. Park here. The foot trail has been closed due to erosion, so bushwhacking through manzanita and poison oak may be necessary but definitely not suggested. From the intersection, turn right on McCullough toward the signs to Rodeo Beach. Take the first dirt trail on your right, and then follow a not-so-good foot trail on your right less than 10 yards from the paved road. This meanders 35 yards up the hill to Genocide Rock.

Genocide Rock, Marin County

SUPER SLAB

This chunk of blue schist has a myriad of very difficult boulder problems, the majority of them require loads of power. Most problems are in the V6-V9 range; but if you walk around to the east-facing side, you will notice a small section of vertical rock with easier problems ranging from V0 to V3. The short walk from CA 1 calls for long pants due to the over abundance of poison oak.

The bouldering rock was discovered by North Bay climber Mark Howe in the early 1990s. He scoped out the south side of the rock more thoroughly than the north side though and missed most of the worthy bouldering possibilities. A few years later, Howe's friend Chris Summit re-discovered the rock, setting and naming more than a dozen problems.

Super Slab is almost entirely blue schist, an extremely hard dense rock. If you look closely at this schist, you will notice it has tiny pockmarks covering most sections. Until recently these holes were filled with tiny garnets, some of which can still be found on the rock or the ground, but most have fallen out over time or been picked out and carted away by people.

This schist was originally mudstone or sandstone, which was later metamorphosed. During its formation, it was taken at least 10 kilometers below the surface and then brought back up. Interestingly enough, the original bedding of the sedimentary rocks is still intact even after the huge transformation.

Directions: Head north from the gas station in Jenner, on the east side of CA 1, and go 1.1 miles to a turnout on the west side of the road. The rock is not visible if you are driving north but very apparent if you are traveling south. Cross the highway and walk about 25 yards to a trail that goes up to the visible slab, 30 yards up the hill.

Super Slab, Mendocino County

Lucas Valley Preserve/Marinwood Rock, Marin County

LUCAS VALLEY PRESERVE/MARINWOOD ROCK

This 30-foot rock offers a little fun for locals in Marin but really is not worth a long drive. Only one bolted route exists on it, but there are three anchor bolts on top, so other top-roping lines and bolted routes are possible if the rock is cleaned. The sport route has three bolts and is a 5.11d. It is a fun bouldery route with the crux just below the top. Former Marin resident Yeishi Horowitz bolted the route in the late 1990s. This rock is chert and dries quickly after a rain.

Directions: To get to the rock, exit off U.S. Highway 101 in San Rafael/Terra Linda onto Lucas Valley Road. Head west on Lucas Valley for about 2.5 miles and turn right onto Mount McKinley Road. Go two blocks and turn left on Idylberry Road. Drive 3 blocks and turn right onto Red Mountain Road. Park here and walk up the trail that begins at the end of Red Mountain.

Take the foot trail uphill where it merges with a fire road in the Lucas Valley Preserve. Follow the fire road uphill for about 0.25 mile. When you reach a grove of oak trees on your left, you will need to walk off the fire road and onto a small foot trail that leads you across a small grassy field and down into the oak grove. One way to know you are taking the correct trail off of the fire road is that the foot trail to your left begins where an oak tree is close enough to the fire road that its leaves hang over the left (or north) edge of the trail.

The foot trail leading down into the oaks will wind left and then uphill where a few wooden steps will lead you directly to the rock on your left side. From the fire road, it should not take longer than ten minutes to get there.

Climber walking off fire road into grove of oak trees, heading to the Lucas Valley Preserve/Marinwood Rock

Lower Guadalupe Rock, Guadalupe Rocks

GUADELUPE ROCKS

If an earth-shattering quake occurs and decimates Castle Rock State Park and the Skyline Boulevard Slabs, Guadalupe Rock might become a viable climbing option. Otherwise, steer clear of the unpleasant mud and flies at Guadalupe Rock and find a better place to climb. The area consists of three rocks: Roadside Rock, Upper Rock, and Lower Rock. Roadside Rock is the only legitimate climbing spot.

Roadside Rock is easiest to approach and mud is not in the picture. It is 50 feet tall and has three good bolts on top but no hangars. A large tree, 20 feet behind the rock on the hillside, can be slung for toproping. Unfortunately, the bottom ten feet of rock is spray-painted with unimaginative graffiti.

The left side of the rock has blocky climbing from 5.2 to 5.6. The center portion of the rock has harder lines ranging from 5.6 to 5.8. The right side has a small blocky roof section and various lines from 5.3 to 5.9.

As for the two other rocks, the Lower Rock is no longer located on the edge of the Guadalupe Reservoir in Los Gatos; it is in the reservoir. The southwest side of Lower Rock (with the majority of routes) cannot be accessed from the base, unless the climber wants to wade through about four feet of brackish water. The mud that still covers the bottom 20 feet of the rock reveals a water line that is often much higher.

Access to the top of the rock is via the backside by crossing a murky stream surrounded by signs that warn against eating any fish living in the reservoir due to their toxicity. If you do decide to cross the stream to gain access, do not forget your waders. You will be up to your ankles in smelly, mushy mud. There are six

Roadside Rock, Guadalupe Rocks

good bolts on top of the rock. It is possible to lower from the bolts to a height just above the murky depths, then proceed to climb the routes to the top. This option still leaves a lot to be desired since dried mud covers the bottom half of the routes.

In past years, the base of the rock was not submerged, but according to the rangers at Santa Clara County, the base of the rock is now almost always covered in water. This is why the rock is now referred to by many as "Diving Rock," (never mind the obvious question). In addition, although climbing is not illegal, the Santa Clara Valley Water District "discourages use of this rock for both diving and climbing."

The left side of Lower Rock has easy 5.2 lines on it. Just left of center, a 5.9 right-facing flake leads to face climbing. At dead center, there is a 5.10c with a small roof move near the base. And just right of center is another 5.9 crack to face route. The right side of the rock, which is at a lower angle, has a couple lines that go at 5.8 and 5.9.

The Upper Rock is about 75 yards uphill, southwest of the dam. This rock is not visible from the road. In past years, it was on private property, but this land has recently been sold to the Midpeninsula Regional Open Space District (MPROSD). Currently the section of land is closed to the public, and the MPROSD claims citations will be issued to any climbers near Upper Rock. The 40-foot rock has a spattering of routes on it ranging from 5.0 to 5.5.

Directions: Take Interstate 280 (southbound) to Interstate 85 (southbound) in Los Altos. Exit at Camden Avenue, turn right, and drive 1.8 miles to Burke Road. Turn right on Burke and follow the road veering left where it will become Hicks Road. Drive 3.7 miles on Hicks Road to Roadside Rock on your right-hand side opposite the reservoir. For Lower Rock, go 0.7 mile past Roadside Rock. The rock will appear down a hill on your left on the edge of the reservoir.

MAZZONES/BOULDER RIDGE

Mazzones/Boulder Ridge, once a vast boulder field covering almost four acres, was almost completely demolished during the writing of this book. Dozens of sandstone boulders in a myriad of shapes and sizes were strewn across rolling hills in south San Jose. The area was located just off Almaden Expressway, south of CA 85. Hundreds of fine problems are gone, as well as many cracks and toproping routes. A well-manicured golf course with spiraling concrete paths and a few lonely boulders are all that remain.

Mazzones was popular in the 1980s, but with Castle Rock's increased popularity only 14 miles away and ever expanding development across the Silicon Valley, the site acquired more beer cans and used toilet paper than chalk marks on the rocks. What took thousands of years to form and what sat undisturbed for another 10,000 years, took only a few months to demolish and remove. The Santa Clara County Open Space Authority refused to comment or speak about Mazzones/Boulder Ridge and its "development."

The photo included was taken during the area's demise in December 2000, among bulldozers and crews constructing the new golf course. The demolition team was happy to see us leave, and with the depressing destruction all around us, we said goodbye to the few remaining boulders and sailed off for neighboring Castle Rock.

See the photo for Mazzones/Boulder Ridge on page 214.

Chris Summit on one of the last remaining boulders at Mazzones/Boulder Ridge

CLIMBING GYMS

Vertex Climbing Gym
6,000 square feet of
   climbing area
3358 A Coffey Lane
Santa Rosa, CA
(707) 573-1608
climbvertex.com

Class 5 Fitness
7,000 square feet of
   climbing area
25 B Dodie Street
San Rafael, CA
(415) 485-6931
touchstoneclimbing.com

Ironworks
14,000 square feet of
   climbing area
88 Potter Street
Berkeley, CA
(510) 981-9900
touchstoneclimbing.com

Mission Cliffs
14,000 square feet of
   climbing area
2295 Harrison Street
San Francisco, CA
(415) 550-0515
touchstoneclimbing.com

Twisters Climbing Gym
3,000 square feet of
   climbing area
2639 Terminal Boulevard
Mountain View, CA
(650) 969-1636

Planet Granite
14,000 square feet of
   climbing area
2901 Mead Avenue
Santa Clara, CA
(408) 727-2777

Pacific Edge
14,000 square feet of
   climbing area
104 Bronson Street #12
Santa Cruz, CA
(831) 454-9254

Rocknasium
720 Olive Drive
Davis, CA
(530) 757-2902

Pipeworks
12,000 square feet of
   climbing area
116 North 16th Street
Sacramento, CA
(916) 341-0100
touchstoneclimbing.com

Granite Arch
23,300 square feet of
   climbing area
11335 Folsom Boulevard
Rancho Cordova, CA
(916) 852-ROCK

RATED ROUTE INDEX

Technical Climbs

5.2
Approach, Sunset Boulders ★ 50

5.3
Chimney, Butt Rock 114
Cote Memorial Wall ★ 125
Face, Leaning Tower ★ 65

5.4
The Cleavage ★★★ 124
Face Routes, Goat Rock ★★ 152
Face, Northern Formation ★★ 62
Summit Route, Castle Rock 143

5.5
Bat Crack ★★★ 124
Face, Leaning Tower ★★ 65
Face, Leaning Tower ★★★ 65
Face, Sunset Boulders 50

5.6
Beginners Crack, Cragmont ★★★ 96
Bucket Prow ★★★★ 98
Castle Rock Cave ★★★ 116
Charlie Solo ★ 147
Chimney, Castle Rock ★ 143
Crack, Boy Scout Rocks ★★ 110
Crack, Dry Creek Sea Crag ★ 37
Face, Northern Formation ★★★ 62
Freeway ★ 125
Hour Glass ★★ 125
The Interesting Block ★★ 37
Unknown, The Egg ★★★★ 80

5.7
Arête, Plaque Rock ★★ 101
Crack, Boy Scout Rocks ★★ 111
Chimney, Boy Scout Rocks ★★ 113
Chimney, Butt Rock ★★★ 114
Corner, Sunset Boulders ★ 51
Crack to Face, Southern Formation ★★★★ 65
Crack, Dry Creek Sea Crag ★★ 37
Crack, Pinnacle Rock ★★★ 101
The Easy Way Up ★ 193
Face to Crack, Cragmont ★ 96
Face, Boy Scout Rocks 110

Face, The Bubble ★★★ 13
Gutenberger Wall Direct ★★ 193
Left Face, Butt Rock ★ 113
North Crack of Hummingbird Spire (R) ★ 24
Overhang Continuation ★★ 151
The Ramp, Indian Joe Caves ★ 124
Route 4, Northern Formation ★★ 62
Route 5, Northern Formation ★★ 62
The Sandbagger ★★★ 37
Undercling Crack ★★★ 96
Unknown, Skyline Boulder Slabs 169

5.8
Arête, Leaning Tower ★★★★ 65
Arête, Northern Formation ★★★★ 62
Arête, Sunset Boulders ★★★★ 50
Awful Width ★★★ 188
Bandito ★★★ 180
Cave Route, Cragmont ★★ 97
Center Face, Butt Rock ★★ 114
Chamberlin's Chimney ★★ 190
Chockstone, Castle Rock ★★★ 143
Chouinard's Crack ★★★ 109
Crack, Dry Creek Sea Crag ★ 37
Crack, Pinnacle Rock ★★★ 98
Face, Cragmont ★★ 95
Face, Indian Joe Caves ★★ 124
Face, Sunset Boulders ★★ 51
Gutenberger Wall (R) ★ 193
Live and Learn ★★★ 188
Off the Wall ★ 50
The Pillar, Pagoda Rock ★ 119
Route 3, The Far Side ★★★★ 24
Route 4, The Far Side ★★★ 24
Route 7, Indian Joe Caves ★ 125
Route 8, Indian Joe Caves ★ 125
Route 12, The Far Side (TR) ★★ 24
Scorpio ★★★★ 195
Shute-Mills Route ★★★★★ 24
Step to the Left (R) ★★ 25
Table Manners ★★★ 180
Test Piece ★★★★ 190
Theodore Roosevelt (R) ★ 18
Training Pants ★★ 188
Unconquerable ★★★★★ 190
University of Santa Clara
    Practice Climb #1 ★★★★★ 161
Unknown, Skyline Boulder Slabs ★★★ 169

5.9

Amazing Face ★★★★ 113
Bad Bolts 119
The Bear ★★ 20
Crack, The Pit ★★★★ 177
Crack, Dry Creek Sea Crag ★★★ 37
Crack, Sunset Boulders ★★ 50
Cranberries ★ (R) 167
Cranberries Variation 167
Dan's Delight ★★ 188
Dihedral Bypass ★★ 193
Dinkum ★★★★★ 188
Double Cracks, Summit Rock ★★ 161
Egg Face ★★★ 80
Face Routes, Goat Rock ★★ 152
Face, Castle Rock ★ 143
Face, Cragmont ★★ 96
Face, Indian Joe Caves ★★ 124
Face, Pagoda Rock 119
Galapagos ★★★★ 41
Go with the Flow ★★★★★ 180
Kola ★★★★★ 24
The Ladder ★★ 16
Leading to Death ★★ 151
Lichen Us ★★ 193
Lichen Us Variation ★★ 193
Mangler ★★★ 188
The Pile ★★ 24
Rock of Ages Cave ★★ 119
Roe vs. Wade ★★ 177
Route 2, Beaver Street Wall ★★ 131
Route 19, The Far Side ★★★ 24
Saviour Heart (R) ★★★ 24
Seymour Frishberg (R) ★★★ 23
Sidesaddle ★★★★ 181
Slabby ★ 101
South Face of Hummingbird Spire ★ 24
South Face, Indian Rock ★ 153
Sunset Face ★★ 51
Triple Overhang ★★ 151
Unknown, Grey Slab ★★ 79

5.10

Mastophilia ★★★ 195
Route 13, The Far Side (TR) ★★ 24
Unknown, Skyline Boulder Slabs ★ 167

5.10a

Atlas Shrugged ★★ 24
Blowing Bubbles (R) ★★★ 153
Crystal Pockets ★★★ 21
Degeneration ★★ 151
Face, Boy Scout Rocks ★ 111

Face, Boy Scout Rocks ★★ 110
Face, Plaque Rock ★★★★ 101
The Falls ★★★ 147
Farewell to Arms, Castle Rock ★★★ 143
Farewell to Arms, Cragmont ★★★★ 97
Feelin' Your Oats (R) ★★★ 24
Hole in the Wall ★★ 177
Mark's Moderate (R) ★★ 18
No Hands ★ 125
Northwest Face, Pagoda Rock ★ 119
On the Road ★ 16
Overhanging Buckets ★★★★ 98
Pelican Crack ★★★ 50
Puckered Starfish ★★★ 153
Pull Up ★★ 125
Red Wall Face ★★★★ 37
Roof, Castle Rock ★ 143
Route 1, Beaver Street Wall ★★★ 131
Route 5, The Far Side ★★ 24
Rust Never Sleeps ★★★★ 78
Tree Surgeon ★★★ 161
Trigger Finger ★ 180
Wing of Bat ★★★ 177
Yabba Dabba Dudes ★★★★ 116

5.10b

Arête, The Bear ★★★★ 18
Atlas ★★★ 24
Bolt Route ★★★★★ 113
Cave Route, Butt Rock ★★ 113
Chicken Ranch Bingo ★★★★★ 181
Color Coded Quickdraws ★★★★ 181
Corner Route, Mickey's Beach (R) ★★ 73
Crack of Zorro ★ 37
Diagonal Crack, Boy Scout Rocks ★★★★ 113
Face, Cragmont ★★ 97
Face, Leaning Tower ★★★★★ 65
The Great Roof ★★★ 152
Grin and Bear It ★★★ 125
Jeckyl & Hyde (R) ★★★ 16
Moss Ledge ★★★★ 96
Route 3, The Bubble ★★★ 16
Stegosaurus ★★★ 112
Three Fingered Jack ★★★★ 177
Unknown, Skyline Boulder Slabs ★★★ 169
Welcome Mat ★★ 175
Worm Belly ★★ 161

5.10c

A-C Devil Dog ★★★★★ 180
Adhesion (TR) ★★★ 190
The Chief ★★★★ 24
Face It ★★★ 125

Glob of Shit ★★ 161
The Greeboo (R) ★★ 147
Killer Crack ★★★ 50
Mantle Groove ★ 143
Misperception ★ 181
Ort Man Complex ★★ 181
Overhang, Pinnacle Rock ★★ 98
Ozone ★★★★★ 112
P.M. ★★★★ 50
Pebbly Face ★★★★ 109
POS Crack ★★ 151
Prime Directive (R) ★ 177
Rampage ★★★★ 16
The Sea Cave ★★★ 34
Sign Language ★★★★★ 83
Solar Power ★★★★ 13
Viscious Circles ★★★★ 153
Walk a Thin Line (R) ★★★★★ 73
Wayne's World (R) 20

5.10c/d
Old Bolt Ladder, Skyline Boulder Slabs ★★★★
169

5.10d
Better Eat Your Wheaties (R) ★★★ 24
Black Hole Sun ★★★★★ 20
Bolt Filcher ★★★★ 161
Clip, Clip, Wow ★★★★ 181
Dihedral Direct ★★★★ 193
Face, Cragmont (R) ★★ 96
Face, Pinnacle Rock ★★★★ 98
Jungle Book ★★★★ 110
Little Roof ★★ 37
On the Edge ★★★ 125
Ozone Direct ★★★★★ 112
Rackless Crack ★★★★★ 34
Rawhide ★★★★★ 180
Route 3, Beaver Street Wall ★★★ 131
Route 8, The Bubble ★★ 16
Unknown, Skyline Boulder Slabs (R) ★★★ 167

5.10d/11a
Old Bolt Line, Leaning Tower ★★ 65

5.11a
Bear Arête ★★★★ 20
Bearclaw ★★★★ 21
Betty's Beard Right 111
Face ★★★ 125
Keebler's Revenge ★★★ 175
The Molar ★★ 156
The Oracle ★★★ 147

Orange Arête ★★ 125
Putrefaction ★★★ 151
Sport Wall Face ★★★★★ 37
Sunnyside Up ★★ 83
To Pin or Not to Be ★★★★ 180
Uncle Remus ★★★★ 177
Uncle Remus Direct Start (R) ★★★★ 177
Yellow Brick Road ★ 125

5.11b
Aeronautical Engineer ★★★★ 143
The Beast ★★★★★ 16
The Beast Variation ★★★★★ 16
Betty's Beard Left 111
Boneless Chicken Ranch ★★★ 24
Bubble Boy ★★★ 16
Convulsions ★★★ 151
Dinosaur ★★★ 113
Earthling ★★★★ 113
Egghead ★★★★★ 80
Face, Oberman's Rock ★★★ 65
Face, Plaque Rock ★★ 101
Geronimo ★★★ 181
Hocus (R) ★ 153
Moss Critique ★★ 180
Napa Valley Party Service ★★ 20
Oberman's Crack ★★★★ 65
Rectalphobiac ★★★★ 161
Root, Indian Joe Caves ★ 124
Route 4, Beaver Street Wall ★★★ 131
Snake Bite ★★★ 177
War Party (R) ★ 24

5.11c
Bolt Route, Cragmont ★★ 96
Catchy ★★★ 16
Chancroid (R) 161
Crack-A-No-Go Does Go ★★ 114
Dismal Abysmal ★ 153
Donkey Dong ★★★★ 153
Face, Plaque Rock ★★★ 101
Lunge Route ★ 151
Old and in the Way ★ 20
Pie Crust ★★ 110
Sea Breeze ★★★ 50
Swallow This ★★ 175
Unknown, Mickey's Beach (R) ★★★ 73

5.11c/d
In the Buckets ★★★★★ 110
Squeeler ★★★★ 181

5.11d
Above the Law ★★★ 151
Anti-Christ ★★ 147
Clamydia ★★★★★ 151
Ejection Seat ★★★★ 180
Face, Boy Scout Rocks (R) ★★★ 113
Hot Tuna ★★ 77
Krokus ★★★★ 153
Mens Crisis Center ★★ 180
Nancy ★★★★ 77
Route 6, The Far Side ★★ 24
Sidewinder ★★★ 181
Skill Saw Gourmet ★★★★★ 161
Stone Free ★★★★ 20

5.11+
Face, Pinnacle Rock ★★ 98
Roof, Castle Rock 143

5.12
Godzilla (X) 112
Ten Minute Crack ★★★★★ 195
Unknown, Castle Rock ★ 143

5.12a
Bears Choice ★★★ 20
Dwarf Toss ★★★★ 183
High Intensity Discharge ★ 183
Journey to Find the Sun ★★★ 181
Junglework ★★ 81
Kill Uncle ★★★★★ 18
Left Side of Great Roof ★★ 151
Pelicans ★★ 73
Sharky's Machine ★★★ 77
Strip Poker ★★★ 156
Sucka Fish ★★★ 34
Unknown, Mickey's Beach ★ 77

5.12a/b
Grotto Monkey ★★★★★ 183
Kill Uncle Direct Start ★★★★★ 18

5.12b
Cleotitis ★★★ 151
Fingerprint ★★ 190
Flight Simulator ★★★★★ 180
Jason and the Agronauts ★★★★ 18
Sasquatch ★★★★ 183
Spung-Lick-A-Litus ★★ 156
Swallow My Pride ★★★ 18
This is Your Brain on Drugs ★★★★★ 81

5.12b/c
Bohemian Bypass ★★ 34

5.12c
Arête to Left Face ★★★ 125
Little Eiger ★★ 125
Premature Ejection ★★ 180
Sex Porpoises ★★★★★ 78
Shell Shock ★★★ 83
Sturgeon ★★★ 77

5.12c/d
Scurvy ★★★★ 77
Wet Dreams ★★★★ 73

5.12d
Gidget Meets the Turgid Sea Monster ★★★★ 77
Motion in the Ocean ★★ 77
Naked and Disfigured ★★★★★ 77
Pseudo Bohemic Hitchhiking Youth ★★★★★ 37

5.12d/13a
Bombardier ★★★★ 180

5.13a
Holy Mackerel ★★★★ 73
Mutiny ★★ 77
Squid Vicious ★★★ 77

5.13b
Beach Arête ★★★ 77
Dream On ★ 73
Dreams of White Porsches ★★★ 73
Endless Bummer ★★★★ 84
Insomnia ★★★ 73
Judge Dredd ★★★★★ 37

5.13c
Jury Duty ★★ 37

5.14a
Surf Safari ★★★ 84

Bouldering

V0+
Western Traverse   169

V1
Chalupa 45
Sunset Traverse ★★★★ 51
Swiss Cheese 29

V2
Nutcracker 199
Pomo Roof 45
Skyline Boulder Traverse 169

V2/V3
Stonewall Arête 199

V3/V4
Hard Right ★★★ 51

V4
Domino Theory Traverse 163
Hard On Traverse ★★★★ 51
Heavy Metal Traverse 205
Pomosapien Traverse 45

V4/V5
Living A Dream 29

V5
Buttcracker 199
Fort Rosstafarian 29
Ohaus 45
The Specialist ★★★★ 51
Summit or Plummet (R) 169

V6
Coz Daddy Roof 163

V7
Roadside Traverse 205

V8
Welcome to Whine Country 205

V11
Eco-Terrorist 161

ROUTE NAME INDEX

A

A-C Devil Dog 5.10c ★★★★★ 180
Above the Law 5.11d ★★★ 151
Acid Rock 119
Adhesion 5.10c TR ★★★ 190
Aeronautical Engineer 5.11b ★★★★ 143
Amazing Face 5.9 ★★★★ 113
Anti-Christ 5.11d ★★ 147
Approach, Sunset Boulders 5.2 ★ 50
Are You Experienced Boulder 87
Arête, The Bear 5.10b ★★★★ 18
Arête, Leaning Tower 5.8 ★★★★ 65
Arête, Northern Formation 5.8 ★★★★ 62
Arête, Plaque Rock 5.7 ★★ 101
Arête, Sunset Boulders 5.8 ★★★★ 50
Atlas 5.10b ★★★ 24
Atlas Shrugged 5.10a ★★ 24
Awful Width 5.8 ★★★ 188

B

Bad Bolts 5.9 119
Bandito 5.8 ★★★ 180
Bat Crack 5.5 ★★★ 124
Beach Arête 5.13b ★★★ 77
The Bear 16
The Bear 5.9 ★★ 20
Bear Arête 5.11a ★★★★ 20
Bearclaw 5.11a ★★★★ 21
Bears Choice 5.12a ★★★ 20
The Beast 5.11b ★★★★★ 16
Beaver Street Wall 127
Beginners Crack, Cragmont 5.6 ★★★ 96
Berkeley Areas 89
Better Eat Your Wheaties 5.10d R ★★★ 24
Betty's Beard Left 5.11b 111
Betty's Beard Right 5.11a 111
Black Hole Sun 5.10d ★★★★★ 20
Blowing Bubbles 5.10a R ★★★ 153
Bohemian Bypass 5.12b/c ★★ 34
Bolt Filcher 5.10d ★★★★ 161
Bolt Route, Boy Scout Rocks 5.10b ★★★★★ 113
Bolt Route, Cragmont 5.11c ★★ 96
Bombardier 5.12d/13a ★★★★ 180
Boneless Chicken Ranch 5.11b ★★★ 24
Boulder Ridge 213
Boy Scout Rocks 108
    East Face of Lower Tier 112
    North Face
        Lower Tier 111
        Middle Tier 111

    Upper Tier 109
    West Face of Middle Tier 110
The Bubble 13
Bubble Boy 5.11b ★★★ 16
Buck's Bar Dome 188
Bucket Prow 5.6 ★★★★ 98
Butt Rock 113
    North Face 114
    South Face 113
    West Face 113
Buttcracker V5 199

C

California Slab 83
Castle Rock, Pine Canyon 116
Castle Rock, Castle Rock State Park 143
    East Face 143
    West Face 143
Castle Rock Cave 5.6 ★★★ 116
Castle Rock Falls 147
Castle Rock State Park 139
    Bouldering 161
Catchy 5.11c ★★★ 16
Cave Rock 119
Cave Route, Butt Rock 5.10b ★★ 113
Cave Route, Cragmont 5.8 ★★ 97
Cave Wall 183
Center Face, Butt Rock 5.8 ★★ 114
Chalupa V1 45
Chamberlin's Chimney 5.8 ★★ 190
Chancroid 5.11c R 161
Charlie Solo 5.6 ★ 147
Chicken Ranch Bingo 5.10b ★★★★★ 181
The Chief 5.10c ★★★★ 24
Chimney, Boy Scout Rocks 5.7 ★★ 113
Chimney, Butt Rock 5.3 114
Chimney, Butt Rock 5.7 ★ 114
Chimney, Castle Rock 5.6 ★ 143
Chockstone, Castle Rock 5.8 ★★★ 143
Chouinard's Crack 5.8 ★★★ 109
Clamydia 5.11d ★★★★★ 151
The Cleavage 5.4 ★★★ 124
Cleotitis 5.12b ★★★ 151
Clip, Clip, Wow 5.10d ★★★★ 181
Color Coded Quickdraws 5.10b ★★★★ 181
Consumnes River Gorge 184
Convulsions 5.11b ★★★ 151
Corner Route, Mickey's Beach 5.10b R ★★ 73
Corner, Sunset Boulders 5.7 ★ 51
Cote Memorial Wall 5.3 ★ 125

Coz Daddy Roof V6 163
Crack of Zorro 5.10b ★ 37
Crack to Face, Southern Formation 5.7 ★★★★ 65
Crack, The Pit 5.9 ★★★★ 177
Crack, Boy Scout Rocks 5.6 ★★ 110
Crack, Dry Creek Sea Crag 5.6 ★ 37
Crack, Dry Creek Sea Crag 5.7 ★★ 37
Crack, Dry Creek Sea Crag 5.8 ★ 37
Crack, Dry Creek Sea Crag 5.9 ★★★ 37
Crack, Pinnacle Rock 5.7 ★★★ 101
Crack, Pinnacle Rock 5.8 ★★★ 98
Crack, Sunset Boulders 5.9 ★★ 50
Crack-A-No-Go Does Go 5.11c ★★ 114
Cragmont 95
    East Face 96
    Northeast Face 95
Cranberries 5.9 R ★ 167
Cranberries Variation 5.9 167
Crystal Pockets 5.10a ★★★ 21

D
Dan's Delight 5.9 ★★ 188
Danger Boulder 87
Degeneration 5.10a ★★ 151
Diagonal Crack, Boy Scout Rocks 5.10b ★★★★
    113
Dihedral Bypass 5.9 ★★ 193
Dihedral Direct 5.10d ★★★★ 193
Dinkum 5.9 ★★★★★ 188
Dinosaur 5.11b ★★★ 113
Dire Blow 113
Dismal Abysmal 5.11c ★ 153
Domino Theory Traverse V4 163
Donkey Dong 5.11c ★★★★ 153
Double Cracks, Summit Rock 5.9 ★★ 161
Dream On 5.13b ★ 73
Dreams of White Porsches 5.13b ★★★ 73
Dry Creek Sea Crag 31
Dwarf Toss 5.12a ★★★★ 183

E
Earthcling 5.11b ★★★★ 113
The Easy Way Up 5.7 ★ 193
Eco-Terrorist V11 161
The Egg 79
    East Face 80
    North Face 80
    West Face 83
Egg Face 5.9 ★★★ 80
Egghead 5.11b ★★★★★ 80
Ejection Seat 5.11d ★★★★ 180
Endless Bummer 5.13b ★★★★ 84

F
Face It 5.10c ★★★ 125
Face to Crack, Cragmont 5.7 ★ 96
Face, Boy Scout Rocks 5.10a ★★ 110
Face, Boy Scout Rocks 5.11d R ★★★ 113
Face, Boy Scout Rocks 5.7 110
Face, The Bubble 5.7 ★★★ 13
Face, Castle Rock 5.9 ★ 143
Face, Cragmont 5.10b ★★ 97
Face, Cragmont 5.10d R ★★ 96
Face, Cragmont 5.8 ★★ 95
Face, Cragmont 5.9 ★★ 96
Face, Indian Joe Caves 5.8 ★★ 124
Face, Indian Joe Caves 5.9 ★★ 124
Face, Indian Joe Caves 5.11a ★★★ 125
Face, Leaning Tower 5.3 ★ 65
Face, Leaning Tower 5.5 ★★ 65
Face, Leaning Tower 5.5 ★★★ 65
Face, Leaning Tower 5.10b ★★★★★ 65
Face, Northern Formation 5.4 ★★ 62
Face, Northern Formation 5.6 ★★★ 62
Face, Oberman's Rock 5.11b ★★★ 65
Face, Pagoda Rock 5.9 119
Face, Pinnacle Rock 5.10d ★★★★ 98
Face, Pinnacle Rock 5.11+ ★★ 98
Face, Plaque Rock 5.10a ★★★★ 101
Face, Plaque Rock 5.11b ★★ 101
Face, Plaque Rock 5.11c ★★★ 101
Face, Sunset Boulders 5.5 50
Face, Sunset Boulders 5.8 ★★ 51
The Falls 5.10a ★★★ 147
The Far Side 21
Farewell to Arms, Castle Rock 5.10a ★★★ 143
Farewell to Arms, Cragmont 5.10a ★★★★ 97
Feelin' Your Oats 5.10a R ★★★ 24
Fingerprint 5.12b ★★ 190
Flight Simulator 5.12b ★★★★★ 180
Flintstone Rock 116
Fort Ross Boulders 27
Fort Rosstafarian V5 29
Freeway 5.6 ★ 125

G
Galapagos 5.9 ★★★★ 41
Genocide Rock 206
Geronimo 5.11b ★★★ 181
Gidget Meets the Turgid Sea Monster 5.12d
    ★★★★ 77
Glen Canyon 133
Glen Canyon Boulders 133
Glob of Shit 5.10c ★★ 161
The Globule 152

Go with the Flow 5.9 ★★★★★ 180
Goat Rock, Castle Rock Falls 151
Goat Rock, Sunset Boulders 47
Godzilla 5.12 X 112
Granite Cove 195
The Great Roof 5.10b ★★★ 152
The Greeboo 5.10c R ★★ 147
Grey Slab 78
Grin and Bear It 5.10b ★★★ 125
Grizzly Caves 102
Grizzly Peak Boulders 101
The Grotto 171
Grotto Monkey 5.12a/b ★★★★★ 183
Guadalupe Rocks 211
    Lower Rock 211
    Roadside Rock 211
    Upper Rock 211
Gunks Revisited 133
Gutenberger Wall 190
Gutenberger Wall 5.8 R ★ 193
Gutenberger Wall Direct 5.7 ★★ 193

H
Hard On Traverse V4 ★★★★ 51
Hard Right V3/V4 ★★★ 51
Heavy Metal Traverse V4 205
High Intensity Discharge 5.12a ★ 183
Hillcrest Boulders 199
Hocus 5.11b R ★ 153
Hole in the Wall 5.10a ★★ 177
Holy Mackerel 5.13a ★★★★ 73
Hot Tuna 5.11d ★★ 77
Hour Glass 5.6 ★★ 125

I
In the Buckets 5.11c/d ★★★★★ 110
Indian Joe Caves 121
Indian Rock 91, 152
    Northeast Face 153
    Southwest Face 153
Insomnia 5.13b ★★★ 73
The Interesting Block 5.6 ★★ 37

J
Jason and the Argonauts 5.12b ★★★★ 18
Jeckyl & Hyde 5.10b R ★★★ 16
Journey to Find the Sun 5.12a ★★★ 181
Judge Dredd 5.13b ★★★★★ 37
Jungle Book 5.10d ★★★★ 110
Jungle Fever 93

Junglework 5.12a ★★ 81
Jury Duty 5.13c ★★ 37

K
Keebler's Revenge 5.11a ★★★ 175
Kill Uncle 5.12a ★★★★★ 18
Kill Uncle Direct Start 5.12a/b ★★★★★ 18
Killer Crack 5.10c ★★★ 50
Klinghoffer Boulders 163
Kola 5.9 ★★★★★ 24
Krokus 5.11d ★★★★ 153

L
The Ladder 5.9 ★★ 16
Leading to Death 5.9 ★★ 151
Leaning Tower 65
Left Face, Butt Rock 5.7 ★ 113
Left Side of Great Roof 5.12a ★★ 151
Lichen Us 5.9 ★★ 193
Lichen Us Variation 5.9 ★★ 193
Little Eiger 5.12c ★★ 125
Little Roof 5.10d ★★ 37
Live and Learn 5.8 ★★★ 188
Living A Dream V4/V5 29
Lucas Valley Preserve 209
Lunge Route 5.11c ★ 151

M
Magoo Boulders 161
Mangler 5.9 ★★★ 188
Mantle Groove 5.10c ★ 143
Mark's Moderate 5.10a R ★★ 18
Mastophilia 5.10 ★★★ 195
Mazzones 213
Meatball Rock 57
Mens Crisis Center 5.11d ★★ 180
Mickey's Beach 69
    Bouldering 84
    East Face 73
    West Face 77
Midway Rocks 195
Misperception 5.10c ★ 181
The Molar 5.11a ★★ 156
Mortar Rock 93
Moss Critique 5.11b ★★ 180
Moss Ledge 5.10b ★★★★ 96
Motion in the Ocean 5.12d ★★ 77
Mount Diablo State Park 105
Mount St. Helena 9
Mount Tamalpais 59
Mutiny 5.13a ★★ 77

N

Naked and Disfigured 5.12d ★★★★★ 77
Nancy 5.11d ★★★★ 77
Napa Valley Party Service 5.11b ★★ 20
Nat's Lyback 93
Nat's Traverse 93
Nature Nazi Boulders 164
No Hands 5.10a ★ 125
North Crack, Hummingbird Spire 5.7 R ★ 24
Northern Formation 62
Northwest Face, Pagoda Rock 5.10a ★ 119
Nutcracker V2 199

O

Oberman's Crack 5.11b ★★★★ 65
Off the Wall 5.8 ★ 50
Ohaus V5 45
Old and in the Way 5.11c ★ 20
Old Bolt Ladder 5.10c/d ★★★★ 169
Old Bolt Line 5.10d/11a ★★ 65
On the Edge 5.10d ★★★ 125
On the Road 5.10a ★ 16
The Oracle 5.11a ★★★ 147
Orange Arête 5.11a ★★ 125
Orange Budda Boulder 87
Ort Man Complex 5.10c ★★ 181
Ort Wall 181
Overhang Continuation 5.7 ★★ 151
Overhang, Pinnacle Rock 5.10c ★★ 98
Overhanging Buckets 5.10a ★★★★ 98
Ozone 5.10c ★★★★★ 112

P

P.M. 5.10c ★★★★ 50
Pagoda Rock 119
Parking Lot Boulder 163
Pebbly Face 5.10c ★★★★ 109
Peeper Rock 79
Pelican Crack 5.10a ★★★ 50
Pelicans 5.12a ★★ 73
Pie Crust 5.11c ★★ 110
The Pile 5.9 ★★ 24
The Pillar, Pagoda Rock 5.8 ★ 119
Pine Canyon 114
Pinnacle Rock 98
The Pit 177
    Lower Main Wall 177
    Upper Main Wall 180
Plaque Rock 101
Pomo Indian Boulders 43
Pomo Roof V2 45
Pomosapien Traverse V4 45

POS Crack 5.10c ★★ 151
Premature Ejection 5.12c ★★ 180
Prime Directive 5.10c R ★ 177
Pseudo Bohemic Hitchhiking Youth 5.12d
    ★★★★★ 37
Puckered Starfish 5.10a ★★★ 153
Pull Up 5.10a ★★ 125
Putah Creek Boulders 201
Putrefaction 5.11a ★★★ 151
Pyramid Rock 163

Q

The Quarry 25

R

Rackless Crack 5.10d ★★★★★ 34
The Ramp, Indian Joe Caves 5.7 ★ 124
Rampage 5.10c ★★★★ 16
Rawhide 5.10d ★★★★★ 180
Rectalphobiac 5.11b ★★★★ 161
Red Wall Face 5.10a ★★★★ 37
Remillard Park 97
Right Face, Butt Rock 5.8 ★★ 114
Ring Mountain 52
Roadside Rock 211
Roadside Traverse V7 205
Rock Lobster 77
Rock of Ages Cave 5.9 ★★ 119
Roe vs. Wade 5.9 ★★ 177
Roof, Castle Rock 5.10a ★ 143
Roof, Castle Rock 5.11+ 143
Roof, Indian Joe Caves 5.11b ★ 124
Rust Never Sleeps 5.10a ★★★★ 78

S

The Sandbagger 5.7 ★★★ 37
Sasquatch 5.12b ★★★★ 183
Saviour Heart 5.9 R ★★★ 24
Scorpio 5.8 ★★★★ 195
Scurvy 5.12c/d ★★★★ 77
Sea Breeze 5.11c ★★★ 50
The Sea Cave 5.10c ★★★ 34
Sex Porpoises 5.12c ★★★★★ 78
Seymour Frishberg 5.9 R ★★★ 23
Sharky's Machine 5.12a ★★★ 77
Shell Shock 5.12c ★★★ 83
Sign Language 5.10c ★★★★★ 83
Skill Saw Gourmet 5.11d ★★★★★ 161
Skull Rock 102
Shute-Mills Route 5.8 ★★★★★ 24
Sidesaddle 5.9 ★★★★ 181
Sidewinder 5.11d ★★★ 181

Skyline Boulder 169
Skyline Boulder Slabs 167
Skyline Boulder Traverse V2 169
Skyline Boulevard Slabs 165
Slabby 5.9 ★ 101
Snake Bite 5.11b ★★★ 177
Solar Power 5.10c ★★★★ 13
South Face, Hummingbird Spire 5.9 ★ 24
South Face, Indian Rock 5.9 ★ 153
Southern Formation 65
The Specialist V5 ★★★★ 51
Split Rock 56
Sport Wall Face 5.11a ★★★★★ 37
Spung-Lick-A-Litus 5.12b ★★ 156
Squeeler 5.11c/d ★★★★ 181
Squid Vicious 5.13a ★★★ 77
Stegosaurus 5.10b ★★★ 112
Step to the Left 5.8 R ★★ 25
Stinsom Beach Boulders 86
Stone Free 5.11d ★★★★ 20
Stonewall Arête V2/V3 199
Strip Poker 5.12a ★★★ 156
Struggler Cliff 193
Sturgeon 5.12c ★★★ 77
Sucka Fish 5.12a ★★★ 34
Summit or Plummet V5 R 169
Summit Rock 156
Sunnyside Up 5.11a ★★ 83
Sunset Boulders 47
Sunset Face 5.9 ★★ 51
Sunset Traverse V1 ★★★★ 51
Super Slab 207
Surf Safari 5.14a ★★★ 84
Swallow My Pride 5.12b ★★★ 18
Swallow This 5.11c ★★ 175
Swiss Cheese V1 29

T
Table Manners 5.8 ★★★ 180
Ten Minute Cliff 193
Ten Minute Crack 5.12 ★★★★★ 195
Test Piece 5.8 ★★★★ 190

Theodore Roosevelt 5.8 R ★ 18
This is Your Brain on Drugs 5.12b ★★★★★ 81
Three Fingered Jack 5.10b ★★★★ 177
To Pin or Not to Be 5.11a ★★★★ 180
Training Pants 5.8 ★★ 188
Tree Surgeon 5.10a ★★★ 161
Trigger Finger 5.10a ★ 180
Triple Overhang 5.9 ★★ 151
Turtle Rock 57

U
The Unnatural Act 136
Uncle Remus 5.11a ★★★★ 177
Uncle Remus Direct Start 5.11a R ★★★★ 177
Unconquerable 5.8 ★★★★★ 190
Undercling Crack 5.7 ★★★ 96
University of Santa Clara
    Practice Climb #1 5.8 ★★★★★ 161

V
Vacaville Boulders 196
Viscious Circles 5.10c ★★★★ 153

W
Walk a Thin Line 5.10c R ★★★★★ 73
War Party 5.11b R ★ 24
Wayne's World 5.10c R 20
Welcome Mat 5.10b ★★ 175
Welcome to Whine Country V8 205
Welcome Wall 175
Western Traverse V0+ 169
Wet Dreams 5.12c/d ★★★★ 73
Wing of Bat 5.10a ★★★ 177
Woodcrest Boulders 198
Worm Belly 5.10b ★★ 161

Y
Yabba Dabba Dudes 5.10a ★★★★ 116
Yabo Boulders 161
Yabo Roof V5 163
Yellow Brick Road 5.11a ★ 125

About the Author

Tresa Black is a passionate rock climber who lives for seeing the world from above. Whether it's traditional, sport, or bouldering, she is happiest when she's climbing.

A California native, Tresa has lived in the Bay Area for seven years. She has worked as a stuntwoman, falling off buildings and getting pushed down stairs; as a radio reporter in San Francisco, Sacramento, and Stockton; and as a bartender off and on for the last eight years.

Tresa is also a strict vegetarian and an animal rights activist who is frequently bossed around by her ornery pot-bellied pig, Giuseppe.

ACCESS: It's every climber's concern

The Access Fund, a national, non-profit climbers organization, works to keep climbing areas open and to conserve the climbing environment. Need help with closures? land acquisition? legal or land management issues? funding for trails and other projects? starting a local climbers' group? CALL US! Climbers can help preserve access by being committed to Leave No Trace (minimum-impact) practices. Here are some simple guidelines:

- **ASPIRE TO "LEAVE NO TRACE"** especially in environmentally sensitive areas like caves. Chalk can be a significant impact on dark and porous rock—don't use it around historic rock art. Pick up litter, and leave trees and plants intact.

- **DISPOSE OF HUMAN WASTE PROPERLY** Use toilets whenever possible. If toilets are not available, dig a "cat hole" at least six inches deep and 200 feet from any water, trails, campsites, or the base of climbs. *Always pack out toilet paper.* On big wall routes, use a "poop tube" and carry waste up and off with you (the old "bag toss" is now illegal in many areas).

- **USE EXISTING TRAILS** Cutting switchbacks causes erosion. When walking off-trail, tread lightly, especially in the desert where cryptogamic soils (usually a dark crust) take thousands of years to form and are easily damaged. Be aware that "rim ecologies" (the clifftop) are often highly sensitive to disturbance.

- **BE DISCRETE WITH FIXED ANCHORS** *Bolts are controversial and are not a convenience*—don't place 'em unless they are *really* necessary. Camouflage all anchors. Remove unsightly slings from rappel stations (better to use steel chain or welded cold shuts). Bolts sometimes can be used proactively to protect fragile resources—consult with your local land manager.

- **RESPECT THE RULES** and speak up when other climbers don't. Expect restrictions in designated wilderness areas, rock art sites, caves, and to protect wildlife, especially nesting birds of prey. *Power drills are illegal in wilderness and all national parks.*

- **PARK AND CAMP IN DESIGNATED AREAS** Some climbing areas require a permit for overnight camping.

- **MAINTAIN A LOW PROFILE** Leave the boom box and day-glo clothing at home—the less climbers are heard and seen, the better.

- **RESPECT PRIVATE PROPERTY** Be courteous to land owners. Don't climb where you're not wanted.

- **JOIN THE ACCESS FUND** To become a member, make a tax-deductible donation of $35.

The Access Fund

Preserving America's Diverse Climbing Resources
P.O. Box 17010
Boulder, CO 80308
303.545.6772 • www.accessfund.org